KNIT BRAVELY

Adventure
CABLES

Brave New Stitch Crossings and 19 Knitting Patterns

MEGHAN JONES

PALM BEACH COUNTY
LIBRARY SYSTEM
3650 Summit Boulevard
West Palm Beach, FL 33406-4198

STACKPOLE BOOKS

An imprint of Globe Pequot, the trade division of The Rowman & Littlefield Publishing Group, Inc.
4501 Forbes Blvd., Ste. 200
Lanham, MD 20706
www.rowman.com

Distributed by NATIONAL BOOK NETWORK
800-462-6420

British Library Cataloguing in Publication Information available

Library of Congress Cataloging-in-Publication Data

Names: Jones, Meghan, 1982– author.
Title: Adventure cables : brave new stitch crossings and 19 knitting patterns / Meghan Jones.
Description: Lanham, MD : Stackpole Books, an imprint of The Rowman & Littlefield Publishing Group, Inc., [2021] | Summary: "In this exploration of cable knitting, Meghan Jones goes way beyond traditional cables. Instead of stopping the overall patterning of the garment when she reaches the cables, she continues the stitch pattern through the cables, working lace, textures, colorwork, and even cables over top of other cables"— Provided by publisher.
Identifiers: LCCN 2021003968 (print) | LCCN 2021003969 (ebook) | ISBN 9780811739498 (paperback) | ISBN 9780811769433 (epub)
Subjects: LCSH: Cable knitting. | Knitting—Patterns.
Classification: LCC TT820 .J64 2021 (print) | LCC TT820 (ebook) | DDC 746.43/2—dc23
LC record available at https://lccn.loc.gov/2021003968
LC ebook record available at https://lccn.loc.gov/2021003969

⊗™ The paper used in this publication meets the minimum requirements of American National Standard for Information Sciences—Permanence of Paper for Printed Library Materials, ANSI/NISO Z39.48-1992.

First Edition

For Seth, Abigail, Norah, Theodore, and Graeham
YOU ARE MY EVERYTHING.

Contents

PATTERNS

Author's Note

I think my favorite thing about knitting is that there really isn't any one totally right way to do it. The sheer number of methods that abound for any given technique can be staggering, and brilliant knitters are coming up with new creative ideas about how to better refine, explore, and expand the process of knitting every day. I like to think of this book as just such an idea, a way to explore knitting in a new manner and investigate the sliver of a thought I had one day: What if . . . any stitch pattern could be cabled?

I wrote the majority of this book during the early days of the COVID-19 pandemic of 2020, and it was an interesting dichotomy to be writing a book about adventuring while being so undeniably at home. In many ways, I felt like an armchair archaeologist, "adventuring" forth from the security of my own knitting chair and making great strides into the unknown while never truly leaving the house. I had originally intended to visit many of the Washington State cities, towns, and landmarks for which the patterns in this book are named,

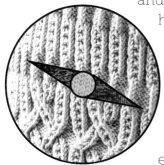

and maybe even take photos there. But with "stay home, stay healthy" measures firmly in place, it became an unreasonable expectation for me to take off and literally travel. So in many ways these unknown places in my own state took on a romantic hue and became my personal interpretation of what that place might be. How might Kitsap, Beacon Rock, or Mt. Shuksan look if I did go there? What did the names make me think of? Looking back at the experience, I am actually rather pleased I could not travel to the real locations and they could become symbolic places representing the mystery of travel not yet taken. An adventure waiting to happen with all the anticipation still intact!

The chapters and the patterns within this book generally increase in difficulty level, beginning with simple crossings and stitches and escalating in challenge level. If you want to explore each pattern with a skill-building focus, then start at the beginning and knit your way through. But in adventuring, fortune favors the brave, and so you may choose to start at the middle or end, halfway up the mountain or partway through the lake. I salute your bravery, acknowledge your wild spirit, and can't wait to see what you make. Please use this book as a stepping-stone, try new crossings, play with texture, color, and form. Take this idea and choose your own adventure!

This book could not have happened without the constant loving support of my husband, Seth. Thank you for listening to all the ideas, planning, self-doubt, and excitement; thank you for making space for my soaring creative process and always being a safe place to curl back up to. You are the one, forever.

Thank you to our children Abigail, Norah, Theodore, and Graeham, who show me how to explore life with passion, humor, love, and unending curiosity every single day. You are the very best moments of my life, and I will always love you with all my heart.

Thank you to my mom and dad, who always support me and all my artistic endeavors.

The greatest of thanks go to Corrina Ferguson, who not only tech edited this book for me but also is an excellent friend and confidante. I also thank Gretchen Cunningham, who happily knit samples and provided constant moral support for finished items. My gorgeous friends who modeled for me: Abbey Crawford, Abigail Jones-Van Eyck, Courtney Clark, Dani Davis, Gerda Porter, Gretchen Cunningham, Ivory Coghlan, Kathleen Cubley, Katie Storo, Kris Rubert, Mimi McClellan, RaeAnn Nolander, and Sarah Magney—thank you for braving the heat, wearing whatever wool I decided to put you in, and sharing your beauty to help my designs shine!

Special thanks to Abigail and Norah Jones-Van Eyck for their photography assistance as well!

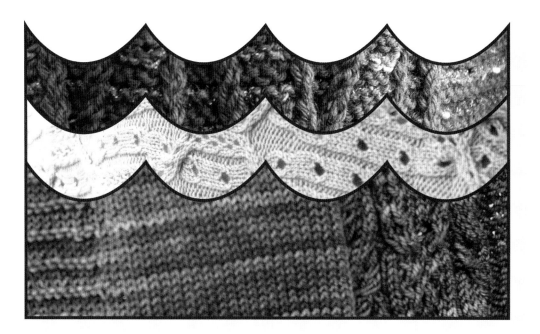

Introduction

The origins of the knitted cable are shrouded in mystery and romance. Tales abound of deep misty mornings filled with tightly knit sweaters mimicking the curving ropes that also adorned the family fishing ships. The story unfolds that each family had a distinctive pattern worked into their knitted garments that ultimately could be used to identify any sailor who could no longer identify himself. A modern spotlight put to these tales has a slightly harsher perspective, with the advent of the knitted cable being more closely tied to marketing geared toward tourists who were more than happy to purchase a handknit sweater if it came with a romantic seafaring yarn. Regardless of their real origins, cables and cable-knit garments have remained popular since they first surfaced in the early twentieth century.

At its core, cable knitting is working stitches out of order, working to the set of stitches you want to move and then rearranging them into a different order before working across them again. The mathematical term for this rearrangement is permutation.

per•mu•ta•tion (noun): a way, especially one of several possible variations, in which a set or number of things can be ordered or arranged.

Traditional cables are primarily worked with a permutation of knit stitches transferred across a background of purl stitches to create the illusion of the knit stitches twisting and moving around each other in the visual forefront of the textile. In classic cables, the set of stitches held to one side of the work with a cable needle is then worked across with only one type of stitch. If more than one type of stitch is worked across the held stitches on the cable needle, then customarily it is likely to again be knit and purl stitches.

But what if they weren't?

Adventure Cables poses these questions:

✳ If cables are simply stitches worked out of order, then why can't any stitch pattern be cabled?

✳ What about taking sets of stitches already in a pattern and moving them across the work as a whole and complete pattern, using texture patterns combined with knit patterns twining around each other, or moving entire colorwork motifs across the work using a cabling method?

✳ What further depth of texture could be achieved by moving these sets of patterned stitches, and how can the graphic design of a lace or colorwork pattern be manipulated by working sections of the stitches in a different order?

This book will give you, the knitter, a path to a brand-new world of reimagined stitch crossings using stitches you may have used before, but never in this format. It includes step-by-step photo tutorial instructions on how to cable with or without a cable needle as well as specific tutorial photos for any unique stitches used and techniques for cabling the Adventure Cables themselves. Each pattern in this book is named after a location in my home of Washington State; some I have visited (many I have not), but all are representative of the adventure that can await us in our own backyard. Think of this book as a visit to summer camp—you probably are never more than a few hours from home, almost everything is familiar, and, although most of the activities might be the same, the experience is bound to be one of a kind. Summer camp is about being led to new experiences, relaxing in the guided activities presented to you, and enjoying the great outdoors. Explore something new, have an adventure, and, most important, be brave!

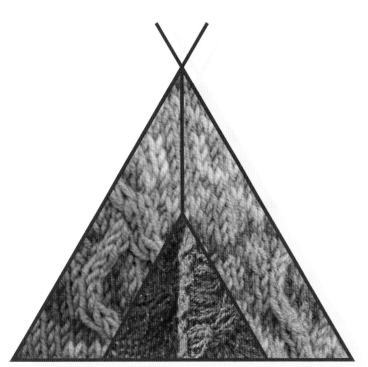

SKILL LEVELS

The patterns in this book encompass a range of knitting skills from intermediate to advanced. The shaping for each garment has been kept simple on purpose to balance the intricate nature of the Adventure Cables with a plain shape and background. Skills that are needed to work patterns in this book are as follows:

- Being able to read a knitting chart (see detailed instructions for this process on page 3)
- Working in the round on circular needles or double-pointed needles
- Working pieces flat and seaming them
- Working short rows for shaping
- Picking up stitches along an edge to work a band, neckline, or sleeve
- Working increases or decreases at the same time as the stitches used in an Adventure Cable pattern
- Working short-row shaping at the same time as or over the stitches used in an Adventure Cable pattern
- Working bound-off stitches at the same time as or over the stitches used in an Adventure Cable pattern

The patterns in this book are arranged into three skill levels that directly correspond to the type of patterning worked during the Adventure Cable. In addition, the patterns are arranged within the chapter in order of difficulty, beginning with the easiest and ending with the hardest. Each pattern has a skill level defined by a small banner stating "Explore," "Adventure," or "Be Brave."

Explore level/Intermediate: These patterns have very simple patterning on the Adventure Cable such as knits and purls.

Adventure level/Advanced Intermediate: These patterns have moderate patterning on the Adventure Cable such as increases, decreases, or slipped stitches.

Be Brave level/Experienced: These patterns have intricate patterning on the Adventure Cable such as crossed stitches or stranded colorwork stitches.

One way to experience this book is to start at the beginning and work through the projects in order; this method will help you get a feel for the Adventure Cables patterning and explore fully the possibilities within these pages. But that said, true explorers never listen to anyone else's plan; they choose a direction and forge ahead toward the great unknown. So follow the path I created or blaze your own—the choice and the adventure are yours!

HOW TO READ KNITTING CHARTS

All Adventure Cables patterning in this book is charted, and written directions are not provided; the very simple reason for this approach is space constraints. When adding cabling into an already established stitch pattern, the number of rows worked evenly between crossing rows is much larger than a regular cable pattern. Extra "breathing" room is needed between crossings to allow the patterning to become visually cohesive before throwing it back across the surface with another crossing. This means that the charts tend to be very long and have many more rows in them than a chart with just cabling, and the space needed to write out all those rows was too extensive. If you are a newer chart reader, take the time to read this overview on charts and make sure to utilize the chart tips located in a box beside every chart.

What Are Charts?

Charts are knitting stitch patterns defined in a grid format, with every box in the grid pertaining to a stitch worked in the fabric. Each grid box contains a symbol that, when deciphered with the stitch key, indicates how to work that particular stitch within the whole pattern.

Numbers on the Side

Where the numbers are placed on the chart indicates whether that chart is worked flat or in the round.

If the numbers are on both the right and the left sides of the chart, then it is worked back and forth, reading the right-side rows from right to left and the wrong-side rows from left to right. This is because when we knit back and forth, we work from right to left across the stitches and then turn the work around to complete stitches on the

Numbers on both sides of the chart mean it is worked back and forth flat in rows.

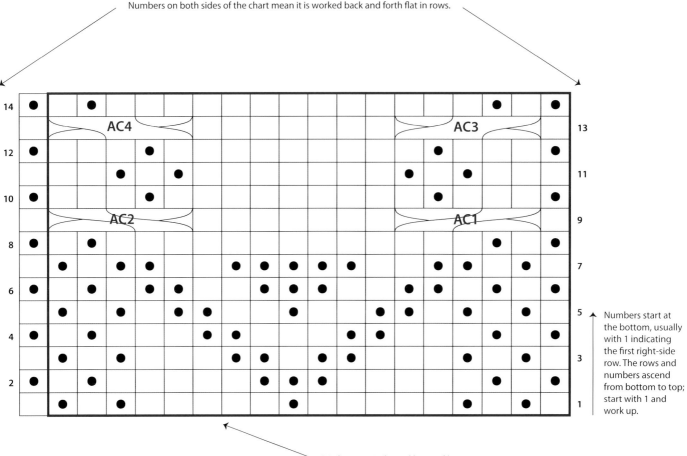

Numbers start at the bottom, usually with 1 indicating the first right-side row. The rows and numbers ascend from bottom to top; start with 1 and work up.

Stitch repeat indicated by a red box

Above is the Adventure Cables Chart for the Thavis Shrug pattern on page 54. Because the numbers are on both sides of the chart, it is worked back and forth. The red box around some of the stitches indicates that you should repeat those stitches the noted number of times before working the last stitch outside the box once.

wrong-side row. Typically the first row is a Row 1 and indicates the right side of the work, also meaning that odd-numbered rows are usually right-side rows and even-numbered rows are usually wrong-side rows.

If the numbers are only on the right-hand side of the chart, then the pattern is worked in the round, and the chart is read from right to left for all rounds of the pattern. This is because when knitting in the round, the stitches are always worked from right to left across the work around and around. For a chart worked in the round, all numbers, whether even or odd, are considered right-side rounds.

Chart row/round numbers are always arranged with the smallest number at the bottom and with the numbers increasing as they ascend the side(s) of the chart. The first row of the chart is always the bottom line of the grid, and subsequent rows are worked from bottom to top. Knitting charts are worked from the bottom up because knitting is essentially worked from the bottom up, as we are adding rows of stitches onto the top of the already created rows of stitches. This rule can be especially helpful to remember when trying to find out what row was worked last—take note of what has already been completed in the knitted piece and try to match it to the chart.

"No stitch" inside a chart is indicated by a gray square; this stitch does not technically exist.

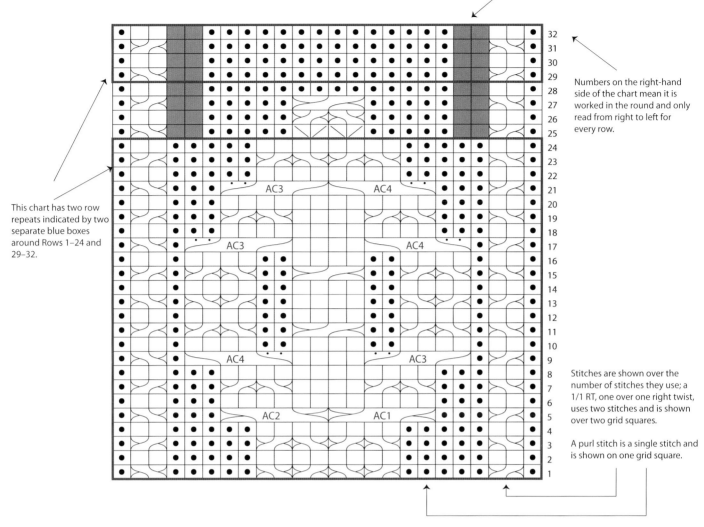

Numbers on the right-hand side of the chart mean it is worked in the round and only read from right to left for every row.

This chart has two row repeats indicated by two separate blue boxes around Rows 1–24 and 29–32.

Stitches are shown over the number of stitches they use; a 1/1 RT, one over one right twist, uses two stitches and is shown over two grid squares.

A purl stitch is a single stitch and is shown on one grid square.

Above is the Adventure Cables Chart from the Roxboro Mittens pattern on page 117. Because the numbers are only on the right-hand side of the chart, this chart is worked in the round, and every chart row is worked from right to left. The blue box repeats indicate that this chart has rows that are repeated. Rows 1–24 are in a box that shows they are worked more than once; Rows 25–28 are outside a box, so they are worked once; and Rows 29–32 are inside a separate box, so they are worked more than once.

Numbers on the Bottom

Numbers on the bottom of a chart indicate the stitch count used for that chart; in this book, the only charts that have numbers at the bottom are charts with straight vertical sides.

Reading the Stitches

Whether working back and forth or only from right to left, each grid section of the chart indicates a stitch and an action to work that stitch with. The grid box itself represents a single stitch, and the symbol within that grid box indicates how that stitch is worked. To actually create the stitches, work across the row horizontally treating each stitch as indicated by the symbol in the corresponding grid square.

Sometimes the symbols can use more than 1 stitch (or grid box) action like decreases or cabling using 2 or more stitches. Decreases are usually noted on the number of stitches they become after the decrease is worked, *not* over how many stitches the decrease uses. Cables are usually noted over the number of stitches that they use, depicting the number of stitches crossing over a number of stitches and in what direction they are moving.

The Key

Each chart has a stitch key (a small box to the side of the chart that defines each of the symbols). Since the key has limited space, those symbol definitions are often abbreviated; further elucidation of the stitches can be found either in the abbreviations at the end of the book or within the notes for each pattern. Typically, standard abbreviations like k (knit), p (purl), or k2tog (knit 2 together) are found within the abbreviations section, and more specific definitions like cable information can be found in the "Pattern Notes" section of the specific pattern.

Stitch Repeat

If the chart has a colored box around a section of stitches, it likely indicates a stitch repeat or a row repeat. In this book, stitch repeats are red and row repeats are blue; they are a visual clue that this section of the chart will be repeated. When working with repeated sections, work the rows or stitches before the marked section once, repeat the marked section as many times as indicated, and work any rows or stitches after the marked section once.

No Stitch

Sometimes a chart contains a gray square called "no stitch." This square is literally a stitch that does not exist. It may have been removed during decreases or it may not exist until an increase in a following row. Regardless, if you come across a "no stitch," skip over it and work the next stitch as indicated by the next filled grid square.

Decreases

Decreases are noted within a chart over the number of stitches that are present *after* the decrease is complete. A cdd (central double decrease) uses 3 stitches but creates 1 stitch, so it is indicated over 1 stitch. If decreases are worked in the center of a chart without accompanying increases, the resulting loss of stitches may be indicated by a "no stitch" square. If decreases are worked on the edges of the chart, the chart will no longer retain its straight vertical edges—a stair-step effect will take place as the stitches on one side or both sides are removed from the work.

Increases

Increases are typically noted over the number of stitches that they create (with the exception of "specialty stitches"—see below). When a chart contains increases for shaping, the vertical side of the chart will alter as more stitches are added to it. When a chart contains increases that are combined with an equal number of decreases, the overall stitch count remains the same; this effect is seen in lace patterning.

Specialty Stitches

Some stitches defy the rule of each stitch using a single grid square when 1 stitch is increased to more than 1 stitch without increasing the number of grid squares used. These types of stitches are noted on the key as a single grid square symbol and are then defined within the Pattern Notes, indicating how many stitches are actually worked. Most of the time the reason for doing this is so that an increase/decrease can happen within 1 stitch to create a decorative effect without disrupting the flow of the whole chart by adding stitches into the middle of the grid.

This set of specialty stitches increases one stitch to 5, then works 5 sts even for 3 rows, and decreases 5 sts to one. This is all indicated over one stitch since the increases and decreases do not shape the chart; they are purely decorative within the patterning.

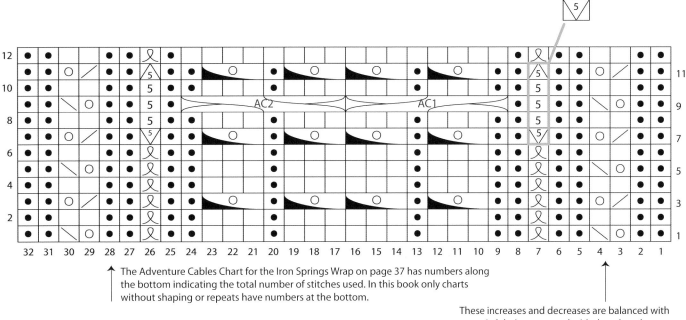

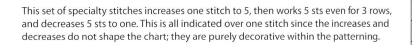

The Adventure Cables Chart for the Iron Springs Wrap on page 37 has numbers along the bottom indicating the total number of stitches used. In this book only charts without shaping or repeats have numbers at the bottom.

These increases and decreases are balanced with one stitch being removed with the ssk and one stitch being added with yarn over. They do not affect the vertical sides of the chart and so are considered lace patterning.

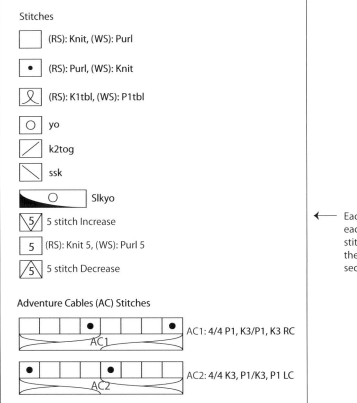

Stitches

☐   (RS): Knit, (WS): Purl

●   (RS): Purl, (WS): Knit

Ⴜ   (RS): K1tbl, (WS): P1tbl

○   yo

╱   k2tog

╲   ssk

◣○   Slkyo

⑤╱   5 stitch Increase

5   (RS): Knit 5, (WS): Purl 5

╱⑤╲   5 stitch Decrease

Adventure Cables (AC) Stitches

AC1   AC1: 4/4 P1, K3/P1, K3 RC

AC2   AC2: 4/4 K3, P1/K3, P1 LC

Each chart has a key that indicates how to work each stitch within the grid. Definitions for these stitches can be found in the Abbreviations list at the end of the book or within the "Pattern Notes" section at the beginning of each pattern.

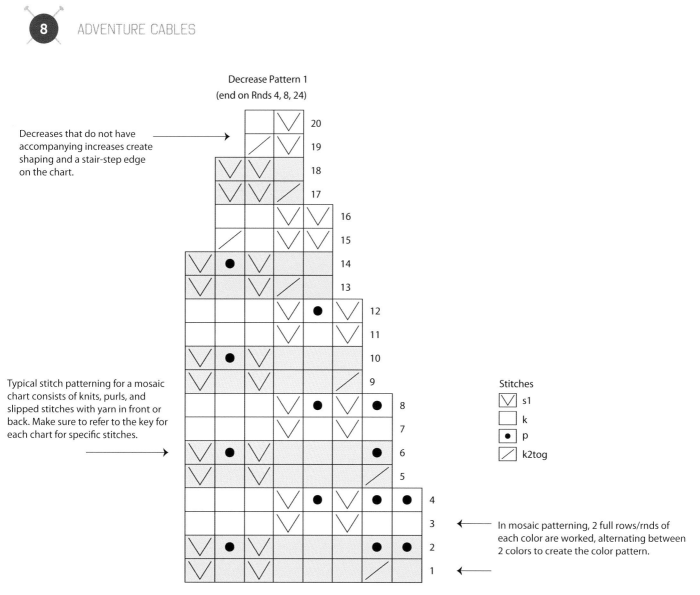

Decrease Pattern 1
(end on Rnds 4, 8, 24)

Decreases that do not have accompanying increases create shaping and a stair-step edge on the chart.

Typical stitch patterning for a mosaic chart consists of knits, purls, and slipped stitches with yarn in front or back. Make sure to refer to the key for each chart for specific stitches.

Stitches

∨	s1
☐	k
●	p
╱	k2tog

In mosaic patterning, 2 full rows/rnds of each color are worked, alternating between 2 colors to create the color pattern.

The Adventure Cables Pattern for the Karamin Hat on page 161 is a great example of a chart that has decreases for shaping. The reduced stitch count created by decreases without increases creates the crown of the hat. This chart also shows the alternating 2 rows of color that is typical for a mosaic patterning chart.

Colors

Typically, colorwork is indicated on a knitting chart by the grid square being completely filled with the color that the stitch should be worked with. In some cases, there is also a symbol in the square. For mosaic patterning, the most common symbols within the colored grid squares will be knit, purl, and slip 1 with yarn in front or back. Mosaic patterning has 2 full rows/rnds of each color in which stitches are either worked or slipped, and only one yarn is used at a time.

Charts for stranded patterning have the color pattern indicated within the grid squares, and sometimes there are also symbols to indicate the different colors. Typically stranded patterning is worked with stockinette, unless the specific chart indicates otherwise. When working a stranded chart, work each stitch using the color indicated by the chart, loosely carrying the other yarn(s) along the back. More than one yarn is used at the same time, and all stitches are worked in a row/rnd.

Tekoa Mittens
Adventure Cables Chart

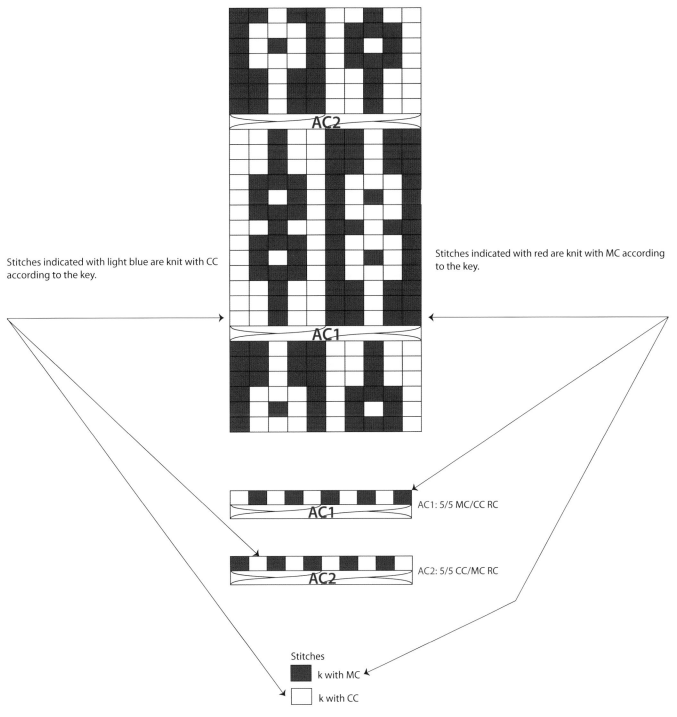

Stitches indicated with light blue are knit with CC according to the key.

Stitches indicated with red are knit with MC according to the key.

AC1: 5/5 MC/CC RC

AC2: 5/5 CC/MC RC

Stitches

■ k with MC

☐ k with CC

HOW TO READ THE ADVENTURE CABLE CHARTS

The charts in this book are unique in that a way was needed to add patterning within a cable without making the chart unnecessarily complicated. To do this, the patterning that will be worked within each cable has been added to a special Adventure Cables key that is located beside each individual chart. Each Adventure Cable is identified by an abbreviation and a number—AC (for Adventure Cable) and a number like 1, 2, 3, and so on—notated in red directly on the cable in the chart. In the key, these cables are shown with the number of stitches in the crossing and the types of patterning worked in order *after* the stitches have been crossed. To read the keys as a chart, the knitter can observe the symbols that are separated and above the cable from right to left, the same as a regular chart. A bracket holds each AC cable with the stitches it should be worked with. The definitions for these Adventure Cables are unique to each pattern and are located at the beginning of each respective pattern within the "Pattern Notes" section. The definitions are written for use with a cable needle and without a cable needle so knitters can choose their preferred method. The labels for the Adventure Cables start with two numbers separated by a slash: 4/2, 2/3, 5/1. The first number tells how many stitches will end up in front after the cable is worked; the second number tells how many stitches will be in back. Other cables that use the traditional combination of knits and purls are noted in the regular key with any other stitches used in the chart.

Each chart also has a "Tips" box that has extra information about that chart such as:

* Worked flat (read from right to left for RS rows, left to right for WS rows)
* Worked in the round (read from right to left for all rows)
* Uses cables worked with knit sts
* Uses Adventure Cables (AC) worked with knit and purl sts
* Uses Adventure Cables (AC) worked with lace sts
* Uses Adventure Cables (AC) worked with slipped sts
* Uses Adventure Cables (AC) worked with stranded sts
* Uses Adventure Cables (AC) worked with cable sts
* Has a stitch repeat; repeat stitches enclosed in red box indicated number of times
* Has a row repeat; repeat rows enclosed in blue box indicated number of times
* Entire chart is repeated indicated number of times
* Chart rows are repeatable for pattern length adjustment
* Chart is repeatable for a larger shawl
* Work each stitch with color indicated within square

These extra tips are to help you, the knitter, understand how that particular chart is supposed to be worked and assist with any alterations you may want to add to the pattern.

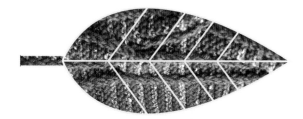

Roxboro Mittens Adventure Cables Chart

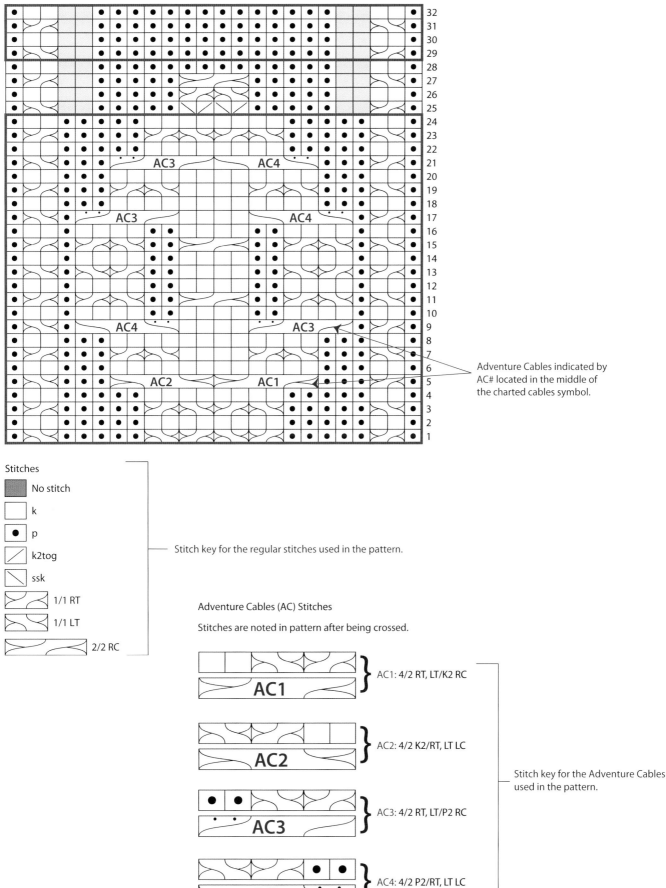

Adventure Cables indicated by AC# located in the middle of the charted cables symbol.

Stitches

(grey box)	No stitch
(white box)	k
●	p
/	k2tog
\	ssk
(symbol)	1/1 RT
(symbol)	1/1 LT
(symbol)	2/2 RC

Stitch key for the regular stitches used in the pattern.

Adventure Cables (AC) Stitches

Stitches are noted in pattern after being crossed.

AC1: 4/2 RT, LT/K2 RC

AC2: 4/2 K2/RT, LT LC

AC3: 4/2 RT, LT/P2 RC

AC4: 4/2 P2/RT, LT LC

Stitch key for the Adventure Cables used in the pattern.

WORKING WITH CABLE NEEDLES

Cable Needles (cn)

Many knitters learned to work cables using a cable needle, a small double-pointed needle sometimes with a curve in it that serves to hold the stitches in the front or the back of the work while working the stitch permutation. Cable needles are especially handy when working a cable crossing with a larger number of stitches, as they can help prevent the knitter from losing those stitches when creating the stitch crossing. Typically cable needles are sold as narrow slippery metal needles with a point on either end; some have a curve in the middle of the needle, and others are bent at a right angle. However, in a pinch any narrow cylinder of moderate strength can be used as a cable needle, with most knitters having a story about the use of a pencil, chopstick, bobby pin, or pen as an effective cable needle at some point or another.

An excellent item to consider when choosing a cable needle is a short 5-inch double-pointed needle, made of bamboo or wood, that is the same size or one size smaller than the needles being used in the project. Since the needles are the same size, or only one size smaller, the stitches will not be distorted by the cable needle. And the bamboo or wood is less slippery than the metal, so the knitter will enjoy the added security of the needle sticking in the moved stitches instead of sliding out to tinkle across the floor right at the crux of the permutation.

Adventure Cabling with a Cable Needle

Standard cabling with a cable needle deals with the first set of moving stitches that is closer to the tip of the left needle and then the second set of stitches, which is farther from the left needle tip. The first set of stitches is placed on a cable needle and held in either the front or the back of the work. Then a set of stitches on the main needle will be worked across before the held stitches are worked across in the intended stitch pattern.

When Adventure Cabling with a cable needle, stitches will be placed on the cable needle and held in the front or the back of the work the same as with regular cabling. The difference is that the stitches on the cable needle and/or the stitches remaining on the left tip will be worked across in a stitch pattern. This stitch pattern may be a texture pattern composed of knits and purls, a lace pattern with yarn overs and decreases, or even a smaller cable pattern. For this reason, it is best to learn both the cabling with a cable needle and cabling without a cable needle to be truly proficient at the Adventure Cables in this book. It is possible to work all Adventure Cables using 1, 2, or 3 cable needles, but it is less cumbersome to learn to work at least one permutation without a cable needle.

As seen in the "How to Read the Adventure Cable Charts" section, the patterning that will be worked for stitches involved in the Adventure Cable is noted above the cables in the specialized key area. Each Adventure Cable is defined in an additional box that indicates working either with a cable needle or without a cable needle. What follows is the Thavis Cardigan Chart example and accompanying Adventure Cables key.

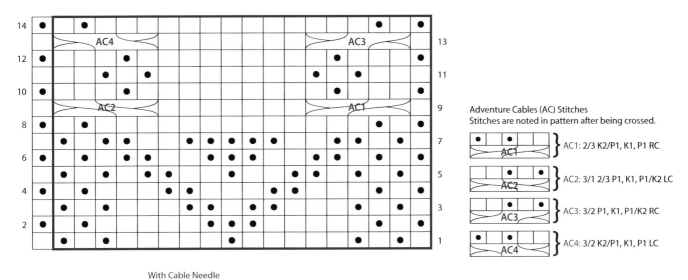

Adventure Cables (AC) Stitches
Stitches are noted in pattern after being crossed.

} AC1: 2/3 K2/P1, K1, P1 RC

} AC2: 3/1 2/3 P1, K1, P1/K2 LC

} AC3: 3/2 P1, K1, P1/K2 RC

} AC4: 3/2 K2/P1, K1, P1 LC

With Cable Needle

AC1: 2/3 K2/P1, K1, P1 RC with cn: Slip 3 sts to cn and hold in back, k2, then p1, k1, p1 from cn.

AC2: 2/3 P1, K1, P1/K2 LC with cn: Slip 2 sts to cn and hold in front, p1, k1, p1, then k2 from cn.

AC3: 3/2 P1, K1, P1/K2 RC with cn: Slip 3 sts to cn and hold in front, k2, then p1, k1, p1 from cn.

AC4: 3/2 K2/P1, K1, P1 LC with cn: Slip 3 sts to cn and hold in front, k2, then p1, k1, p1 from cn.

1. To work AC1 in the Thavis Cardigan Chart using a cable needle, begin by slipping the first 3 sts onto the cable needle, hold them in the back of the work.

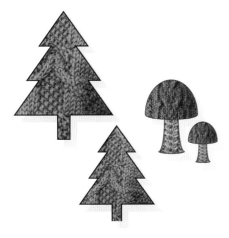

2. Knit 2 sts from the left needle tip.

3. Bring the held 3 sts on the cable needle behind the work back to the left needle tip, making sure that the yarn is not caught between the needles.

4-5. Work across the stitches in pattern, k1, p1, k1.

6. You can see the single purl stitch at the tip of the cable needle below.

LEAVING THE CABLE NEEDLE BEHIND

It is frequently possible (and much faster) to learn to work stitch crossing permutations without a cable needle. Eliminating the step of using the cable needle, putting it down, possibly losing it and looking for it again, over and over, can save a huge amount of time over an entire garment.

When cabling with a cable needle, you are immediately concerned with moving the stitches closest to the tip of the left-hand needle to either the front or the back of the work. They will be held in this position on the cable needle until you are ready to replace them back into the work.

When working without a cable needle, the *opposite* occurs: you will be focusing on the stitches farther in from the tip and whether they will be moving in front of or behind the stitches at the tip. In essence, this method reverses the directions that are provided for cabling with a cable needle.

For example, a 2-over-2 left cross with a cable needle would read like this: Slip 2 stitches onto cable needle and hold in front, knit 2 from needle, knit 2 from cable needle. This essentially takes stitches 1 and 2 out of the work and holds them in front while you are working stitches 3 and 4, and then you work stitches 1 and 2 off the cable needle.

But when this is worked without a cable needle, you are going to focus on stitches 3 and 4; they are the stitches you will move first. To move them, you will reach the tip of the right needle either in front of or behind the work to grab those stitches and rearrange the order. When you slip the needle into those inner stitches, you are going to be slipping all stitches for that cable crossing off the needle, bringing the left tip to the opposite side and reinserting the live stitches back onto the left needle. The best way to have success with this maneuver is to pinch the work to keep those live stitches stable and prevent them from unraveling.

Adventure Cabling without a Cable Needle

Working Adventure Cables without a cable needle is essentially the same process as working a regular cable without a cable needle. First you will rearrange the stitches so that they are in the new order to complete the Adventure Cable, and then you will work across the stitches in the rearranged pattern according to the Adventure Cable key located beside the chart. In the definitions

for cabling without a cable needle, the instructions indicate which side of the work to bring the right needle tip to and then how many stitches to cross over in which direction as seen from the front of the work. These definitions are always written as seen from the front of the work; this may mean that you are moving 1 stitch from the back to create the desired cable direction and stitch count on the front.

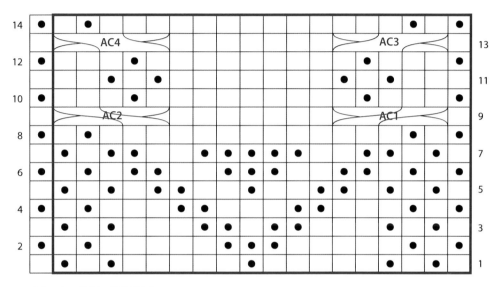

Adventure Cables (AC) Stitches
Stitches are noted in pattern after being crossed.

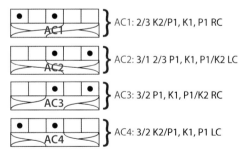

AC1: 2/3 K2/P1, K1, P1 RC

AC2: 3/1 2/3 P1, K1, P1/K2 LC

AC3: 3/2 P1, K1, P1/K2 RC

AC4: 3/2 K2/P1, K1, P1 LC

Without Cable Needle

AC1: 2/3 K2/P1, K1, P1 RC without cn: Reach right needle tip in front of work and insert into the 4th and 5th sts from left tip, slide all 5 sts off left tip, reinsert left tip into first 3 sts behind work, slide 2 sts from right tip back to left tip, k2, p1, k1, p1.

AC2: 2/3 P1, K1, P1/K2 LC without cn: Reach right needle tip behind work and insert into the 3rd, 4th, and 5th sts from left tip, slide all 5 sts off left tip, reinsert left tip into first 2 sts in front of work, slide 3 sts from right tip back to left tip, p1, k1, p1, k2.

AC3: 3/2 P1, K1, P1/K2 RC without cn: Reach right needle tip in front of work and insert into the 3rd, 4th, and 5th sts from left tip, slide all 5 sts off left tip, reinsert left tip into first 2 sts behind work, slide 2 sts from right tip back to left tip, p1, k1, p1, k2.

AC4: 3/2 K2/P1, K1, P1 LC without cn: Reach right needle tip behind work and insert into the 4th and 5th sts from left tip, slide all 5 sts off left tip, reinsert left tip into first 3 sts in front of work, slide 2 sts from right tip back to left tip, k2, p1, k1, p1.

To work AC1 in the Thavis Cardigan Chart without a cable needle:

1. Bring the right needle tip in front of the work and insert into the 4th and 5th sts from the end of the needle.

2. Slip the first 3 sts off the needle while bringing the 4th and 5th sts fully onto the right tip.

3. Bring the left needle tip around the back of the work and reinsert it into the 1st, 2nd, and 3rd sts that were slipped off and are now live.

4. You now have the 4th and 5th sts on the right needle tip and the 1st, 2nd, and 3rd sts on the left needle tip.

5. Slip the 4th and 5th sts back to the left needle tip; you now have the rearranged sts on the left needle tip ready to work.

6. K2, p1, k1, p1 from the 5 crossed sts on the left needle tip.

GAUGE, ALTERATIONS, AND SIZING

A Note on Gauge

Many of the stitch crossings in this book use 4, 6, or even 8 stitches crossed over each other. This high number of stitches being rearranged within the work affects the gauge of the knitted item. It is essential to work a gauge swatch before beginning a project and to block the swatch in exactly the same manner that you intend to treat the finished item. If you are using non-superwash yarn, you should gently wash the swatch in a wool wash and lay flat to dry. Superwash yarn should be laundered according to the manufacturer's guidelines on the label. I personally like to hand wash superwash yarns and then tumble dry on the lowest setting until just barely damp and lay flat to completely dry.

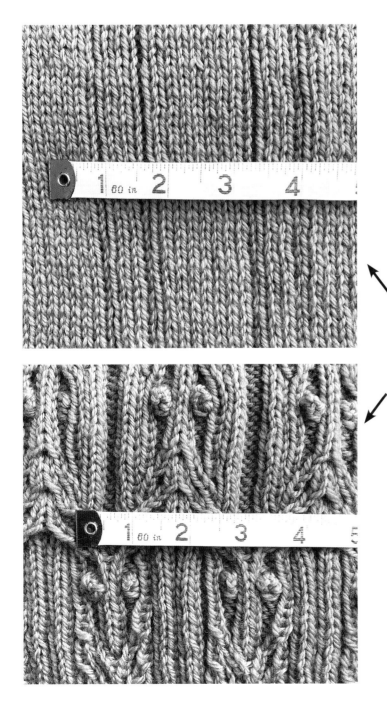

The Point Defiance Pullover has a massive difference in gauge that is addressed by working a decrease row between the Adventure Cables Patterning section and the Upper Body section.

The Upper Body section is worked at a gauge of 22 sts and 26 rows = 4 in./10 cm in the recommended needle size of US7/4.5mm.

By contrast, the Adventure Cables section is worked at 32 sts per 4 in./10 cm (this gauge is noted in the pattern as 20 sts = 2½ in./6.4 cm since the Adventure Cables stitch repeat is 20 stitches wide).

Simply swatching one of these patterns will not give an accurate gauge for the entire project since they are of such disparate sizes.

Additionally, it is important to knit a gauge swatch for the stockinette or garter stitch patterning that will be used on the sleeves or other areas of the garment or shawl. The gauge for the Adventure Cables patterning and the stockinette or other simpler patterning in a project can differ drastically. Working a gauge swatch in each pattern will save time and heartache since it will result in a better project!

Gauge for a sweater is based on the number of stitches that are present within an inch of knitting. A written knitting pattern is based on this number of stitches and requires *exactly* that number for the pattern to turn out at the stated size. For this reason, getting a gauge that is *close* to the right size will get you a garment that is *close* to the right size, but not necessarily a garment that fits. Take the time to experiment with different needle sizes (or even different needle materials) to actually get the right gauge.

Gauge tip: Metal needles are slippery, and knitters tend to tighten their gauge when using them. Bamboo or wooden needles are stickier, so knitters tend to loosen their gauge when working with them. You can use this effect to your advantage if simply changing the needle size doesn't achieve the desired gauge!

Substituting Gauge

If you have swatched on many different needle sizes using the recommended yarn and can't get the noted gauge, you can always see whether your gauge will produce an item in the size you require while working an *alternate size* in the pattern. To do this, take the number of cast-on stitches for the next size higher or lower and divide it by the stitches per inch you have achieved in the swatch. If this number comes closer to the size you desire than the original size, then work the stitches as indicated for your alternate size and the length as indicated by

your original size. Take a pencil and circle the number for each of these throughout the pattern; doing so will help you keep track of the correct size as you work and know what you altered if you come back to the pattern at a later date.

Alterations and Sizing

Many of the patterns in this book are easily altered; any pertinent alteration information for each pattern can be found in the "Pattern Notes" section. This may be a tip on how to add or subtract repeats for a shawl or how to substitute alternate shaping for the sleeves or main body of a garment.

This book includes bust circumference sizes up to 70 in./178 cm; all sizes are written to fit actual bust circumferences with a few inches of ease. This means that the upper-arm circumference, neck, and back width are consistent with plus sizes for the larger finished bust sizes.

Body Length

Many of the garments in this book are written with the same body length (or only slightly different body lengths) for each size regardless of the bust circumference. The size differences for length are worked into the armhole depth; make sure you measure your body from shoulder to hem and subtract the armhole depth to determine the body length you need.

Sleeves: Substitutions and Alterations

Upper-arm circumference is an area that can have a large variation for women. The patterns in this book assume a final upper-arm circumference that tops out at approximately 21 in./53 cm for the largest sizes. However, since no one size fits all, many of the sleeves can be modified for a larger or smaller upper-arm circumference and total length.

Drop-Shoulder Modifications for Kitsap Pullover, Enchantment Lake Cardigan, Point Defiance Pullover, and Seven Bays Cardigan

Drop-shoulder shaping means that there is no armhole shaping; the armholes are worked straight for a length that is equal to half the upper-arm circumference (plus ease). The sleeves for these armholes are then picked up (see "How to Pick Up Stitches around an Armhole" on page 21) and worked in the round from the top down using decreases to taper the circumference to the wrist. Since there is no armhole shaping, changing the upper arm circumference of the pattern is as easy as dividing the required upper-arm circumference by 2 and working the armhole opening to that depth.

Because the shoulder of the sweater drops down onto the upper arm, the length of the sleeve needs to be the total length from the center back to the cuff minus half of the sweater back width.

Drop-shoulder shaping means that there are no decreases at the armhole. The upper body is worked evenly from armhole depth to shoulder.

This type of shaping is less fitted and more relaxed; it also has part of the shoulder "drop" down onto the upper arm—thus the name "drop shoulder."

This type of shoulder is the easiest to adjust, as creating a larger or smaller upper-arm circumference is as simple as working more or less length in the armhole area.

The upper-arm circumference for the sleeves on a drop shoulder will be 2 times the armhole depth.

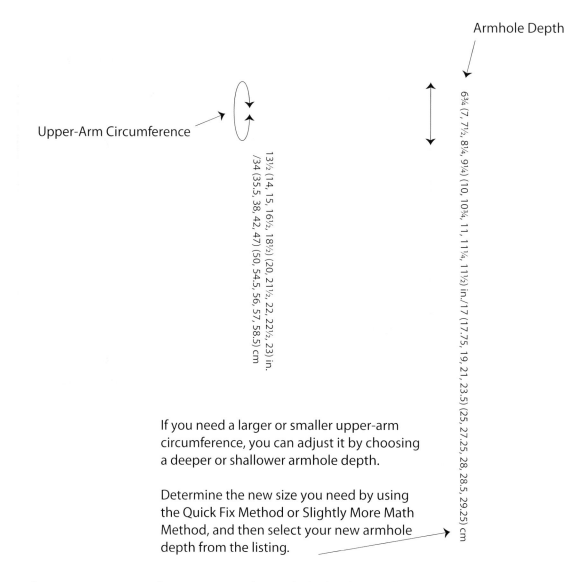

Armhole Depth

Upper-Arm Circumference

13½ (14, 15, 16½, 18½) (20, 21½, 22, 22½, 23) in. /34 (35.5, 38, 42, 47) (50, 54.5, 56, 57, 58.5) cm

6¾ (7, 7½, 8¼, 9¼) (10, 10¾, 11, 11¼, 11½) in./17 (17.75, 19, 21, 23.5) (25, 27.25, 28, 28.5, 29.25) cm

If you need a larger or smaller upper-arm circumference, you can adjust it by choosing a deeper or shallower armhole depth.

Determine the new size you need by using the Quick Fix Method or Slightly More Math Method, and then select your new armhole depth from the listing.

The upper-arm circumference is twice the armhole depth on a drop-shoulder sweater

Armhole Depth: 6 ¾ (7, 7 ½, 8 ¼, 9 ¼) (10, 10 ¾, 11, 11 ¼, 11 ½) in./17 (17.75, 19, 21, 23.5) (25, 27.25, 28, 28.5, 29.25) cm

Armhole Depth X 2 = Upper-Arm Circumference

Upper-Arm Circumference: 13 ½ (14, 15, 16 ½, 18 ½) (20, 21 ½, 22, 22 ½, 23) in./34 (35.5, 38, 42, 47) (50, 54.5, 56, 57, 58.5) cm

Quick Fix Method: Take your upper-arm circumference and divide it by 2; now see which armhole depth in the pattern matches that measurement most closely.

For a looser sleeve, choose ½–1 in./ 1.3–2.5 cm larger depth than half your circumference.

For a closer fit, choose 0–¼ in./0–0.6 cm larger depth than half your circumference.

When working the pattern, work the CO, any stitch instructions, and shaping for your intended bust size, but work the arm-hole depth for the new, desired upper-arm circumference. When working the sleeves, work your new desired sleeve size instead of the size written for the bust you chose. If you need to alter the sleeve length, you can add or remove rounds from the beginning of the sleeve before the decreases begin. Check the gauge of each pattern to see how many rounds are within 1 in./2.5 cm and multiply this number by your needed increase or decrease.

Slightly More Math Method: If none of the upper-arm circumferences that are included with the pattern fit you, then write your own like this:

Take your upper-arm circumference and add ease to it: ½–1 in./1.25–2.5 cm for a closer fit, 1½–2 in./3.5–5 cm for a looser fit.

Divide this circumference by 2; work this as your armhole depth (each pattern tells you when to alter this number).

Sleeve pickup = total upper circumfer-ence X stitches per inch = _____

Wrist number = total desired wrist cir-cumference X stitches per inch = _____ (round to make this number an even number)

Kitsap and Point Defiance require an even number of stitches at the wrist.

Total stitches to decrease = total upper circumference sts – total desired wrist sts = _____

Total decrease rounds = total stitches to decreases / 2 = _____

Now determine how long you need your sleeves; do this by taking the measurement from the center of your back neck to your wrist (or where you want the sleeve to end): total length = _____

Raw sleeve length = total length – half the back width of the bust size you chose (this is also one-fourth of the circumference) = _____

Finished sleeve length = raw sleeve length – the length of any cuff patterning = _____

Kitsap and Point Defiance have 2½ in./ 6.5 cm cuff patterning, Enchantment Lake has ½ in./1.3 cm cuff patterning, Seven Bays has 1½ in./3.8 cm cuff patterning.

Rows between decreases = finished sleeve length / total decrease rnds = _____. Find the nearest whole number and work any extra rnds before you begin the decrease shaping.

HOW TO PICK UP STITCHES AROUND AN ARMHOLE

Many of the sleeves in this book are writ-ten from the top down and worked in the round. This eliminates seaming and (in my opinion) makes for a quicker knit. To work the sleeves, you will need to pick up the indicated number of upper arm stitches for the sleeve around the armhole circumfer-ence. Picking up these stitches *evenly* is very important in order to have a well-fitting sleeve without bunching. There is a simple and visual way to figure out this pickup with

a teeny bit of math, some removable stitch markers, and your upper-arm counts.

1. Lay your garment flat. Using a measuring tape, determine the middle of the armhole depth and place a removable marker at this point. You can also fold the shoulder seam to the bottom of the armhole to find the center if a tape measure is not handy.

2. Now find the center of each half and place a removable marker at each (quarter marking).

3. Draw a vertical line with 4 sections in it, just like the sections on your marked sleeve.

4. Divide your sleeve pickup number by 8; chances are excellent that your pickup number will not divide evenly into 8 sections, but choose the closest whole number.

5. Put that whole number into each section, and then add any extra numbers into the sections as evenly as possible; this is your cheat sheet.

6. Now pick up the stitches along the armhole between each marker as indicated by your cheat sheet.

Total sleeve circumference pickup is 72 sts

Half of sleeve pickup is 36 sts

9 sts   9 sts   9 sts   9 sts

4 even sections of 9 sts each

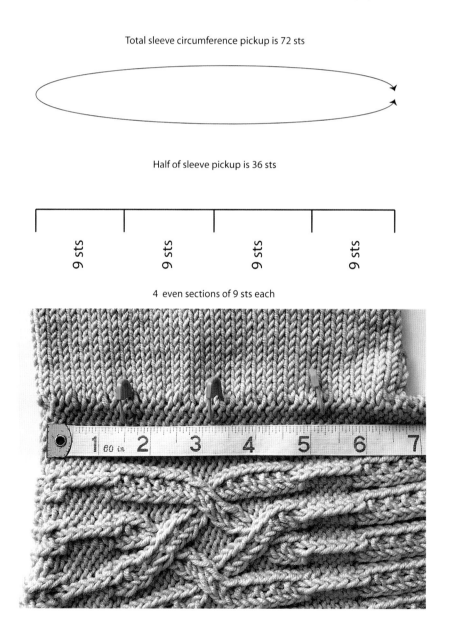

Half the armhole depth for the 48 in./ 122 cm size of the Kitsap Pullover is 7¼ in./ 18.25 cm. By placing one marker in the middle of this depth and two in the middle of each space, the depth can be divided into 4 spaces, each about 1¾ in./4.5 cm.

The total pickup for the sleeve stitches is 72, which is then divided in half to equal 36 stitches on each front and back. This can be further broken down into 4 sections of 9 stitches, which makes for an easy-to-keep-track-of pickup of 9 stitches in each space.

If half the sleeve pickup had been a different number that was not so easily divisible by 4, then you would begin by getting the closest multiple of 4 and placing it in the 4 spaces. Then take any leftover stitches and add them to the spaces. For example, if we are working with the 40½ in./103 cm size of the Kitsap Pullover, our initial sleeve pickup is 60 sts; when divided by 2 for the front and back, we get 30 stitches to divide into 4 sections. Since 30 does not evenly divide into 4 sections, start by dividing 28 into 4 sections of 7, and then add the remaining 2 stitches to alternating sections of 7 like this:

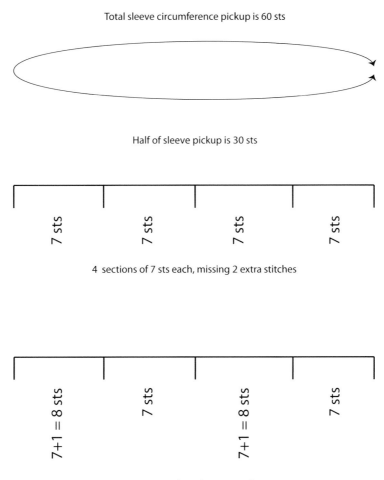

Total sleeve circumference pickup is 60 sts

Half of sleeve pickup is 30 sts

7 sts   7 sts   7 sts   7 sts

4 sections of 7 sts each, missing 2 extra stitches

7+1 = 8 sts   7 sts   7+1 = 8 sts   7 sts

4 sections of stitches to equal 30

Patterns

CROSSINGS WITH

TEXTURE STITCHES

Out of all the stitches available to a knitter, the knit and purl stitches have to be the most versatile. By simply altering the use of these two stitches, myriad texture patterns can be developed without having to learn a new way to insert or wrap the needle. While using knit and purl stitches during cabling is not new, and many cables include crossing knit stitches over purl stitches and vice versa, Adventure Cables take those knit and purl stitches and work them as a pattern that is then crossed into another pattern. This results in a new level of texture, with some of the projects—like the Iron Springs Wrap and the Kitsap Pullover—boasting crisp graphic sections of pattern and texture, while the Beacon Rock Socks and Thavis Shrug have more subtly moving textures that pass in and out of stockinette, garter stitch, and seed stitch.

WHAT TO EXPECT

For the most part, the "Crossings with Texture Stitches" projects use a combination of knits and purls worked over the crossed-stitch sets to move texture across the work. The one exception is the Beacon Rock Socks, in which, although worked with crossing sections of texture, the actual crossing stitches are worked with only stockinette.

SKILL LEVELS INCLUDED

"Crossings with Texture Stitches" is the best place to start Adventure Cables. This chapter includes four projects at an Explore level.

Beacon Rock Socks

Columns of garter stitch and stockinette are crossed over each other in the highly textured Beacon Rock Socks. Cabling takes place over knit stitches for a simple first step into cables using texture—placing texture into the cable but not working the texture during the cable process. The heel and toe are worked with short rows for a totally seamless and stretchy sock.

The cable pattern for these socks was really inspired by trails in the woods. I love how smaller trails seem to flicker and flow with areas of deep texture interspersed with smooth sections. The cushy and seamless garter stitch toe and heel are included for total comfort on tired feet that have just embarked on a new journey.

Explore level/Intermediate: This pattern has very simple patterning on the Adventure Cable such as knits and purls.

Finished Size
6¼ (7½, 8¾, 10) in./15.5 (19, 22, 25.5) cm leg circumference

Socks shown measure 7½ in./19 cm; modeled with 1½ in./4 cm of negative ease. Socks are very stretchy and will accommodate a great deal of ease; choose a size that will result in at least 1½–2½ in./4–6.5 cm of negative ease.

Yarn
Valley Yarns Huntington (#1 super fine weight; 75% superwash merino wool, 25% nylon; 218 yd./199 m per 1.76 oz./50 g): 2 (3, 3, 3) skeins #4150 Red (please note that the second size uses exactly 2 skeins of yarn, and so it is recommended to purchase 3 skeins for that size)

Needles
US size 1 (2.25 mm): set of double-pointed needles (dpns). Adjust needle size if necessary to obtain the correct gauge.

Notions
2 markers (m); cable needle (cn) optional; tapestry needle

Gauge
25½ sts and 27¾ rnds = 2 in./5 cm in Texture and Cables Pattern, unstretched

18 sts and 23½ rnds = 2 in./5 cm in stockinette pattern, unstretched

Pattern Notes

These socks are worked from the top down in the round. The upper leg and top of sock are worked with more stitches than the sole of the sock. The short row heel is worked over the larger number of stitches for a deeper fit, and stitches are decreased for the stockinette sole after the heel is complete. Stitches are decreased on the top of the sock before working the short row toe, and the toe is seamed to the sole on the bottom of the sock.

Stitch Guide

Rib Stitch (multiple of 4 sts)
Rnd 1: *P1, k2, p1; rep from* to m.

Rep Rnd 1 for patt.

3/3 RC using cn: Slip 3 sts to cn and hold in back, knit 3, knit 3 from cn.

3/3 RC without cn: Reach right needle tip in front of work and insert into the 4th, 5th, and 6th sts from left tip, slide first 6 sts off left tip, reinsert left tip into first 3 sts behind work, slide 3 sts from right tip back to left tip, k6.

w&t (wrap and turn): Bring yarn between needles to front of work, slip next st to right tip, bring yarn between needles to back of work, slip st back to left tip, turn work.

Kitchener Stitch: Arrange sts on 2 needles (1 with sole sts and 1 with toe sts); hold needles parallel with toe sts in the front and sole sts in the back and active yarn emanating from front needle (toe sts).

Preliminary steps:

1. Insert tapestry needle into 1st st on front dpn as if to purl, pull through, do not drop.
2. Insert tapestry needle into 1st st on back dpn as if to knit, pull through, do not drop.

Repeating steps:

3. Insert tapestry needle into 1st st on front dpn as if to knit, pull through, drop this st from dpn, insert tapestry needle into 2nd st on front dpn as if to purl, pull through, do not drop.
4. Insert tapestry needle into 1st st on back dpn as if to purl, pull through, drop this st from dpn, insert tapestry needle into 2nd st on back dpn as if to knit, pull through, do not drop.

Repeat steps 3–4 until all sts are used.

Beacon Rock Socks Texture and Cable Pattern

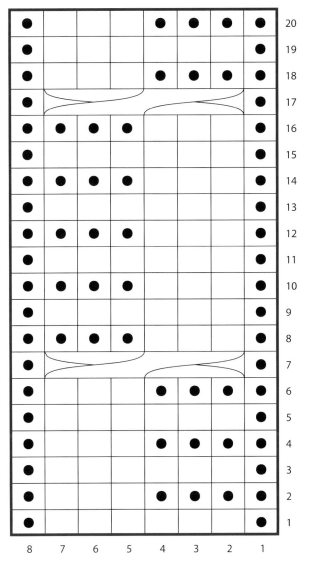

Stitches

☐ k

▣ p

⟋⟍ 3/3 RC

Borders

— Stitch Repeat

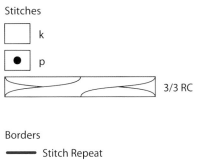

CHART TIPS

Worked in the round (read from right to left for all rows).

Uses cables worked with knit sts.

Entire chart is repeated indicated # of times.

Chart rows are repeatable for pattern length adjustment.

INSTRUCTIONS

Cuff

CO 80 (96, 112, 128) sts using the Old Norwegian method (*see Tutorial on page 39*) or a stretchy method of your choice. Join to work in the round and place marker (pm) for beg of rnd.

Work Rib Stitch (see Stitch Guide) until piece measures 1½ in./4 cm from cast-on edge.

Pattern Setup Rnd: Work the charted Texture and Cable Pattern 10 (12, 14, 16) times around.

Cont in patt as est, progressing through charted Texture and Cable Pattern for 64 more rnds ending on Rnd 5 of patt. 3 repeats of Rnds 1–20 of Texture and Cable Pattern, and Rnds 1–5 are complete. Piece measures 6¼ in./16 cm from cast-on edge; additional length is easily added here but will increase required yardage.

Next Rnd: Work Rnd 6 of Texture and Cable Pattern over first 40 (48, 56, 64) sts (sole stitches), pm, work Rnd 6 of Texture and Cable Pattern over foll 40 (48, 56, 64) sts (instep stitches).

Arrange first 40 (48, 56, 64) sts onto single needle to work heel.

Heel
The short row heel is worked over first 40 (48, 56, 64) sts (sole stitches) using garter stitch; after the heel is completed, stitches are decreased before working sole of sock. Wraps are not lifted or worked in during this garter stitch heel. After wrapping and turning feel free to pull yarn tightly before continuing to knit; this will keep the short row heel neat without gaping holes.

Short Row 1 (RS): K38 (46, 54, 62), w&t.

Short Row 2 (WS): K36 (44, 52, 60), w&t.

Short Row 3: Knit to 1 st before last wrapped st, w&t.

Rep this last short row 23 (31, 39, 47) more times, 12 sts rem unwrapped in center of work, 13 (17, 21, 25) sts wrapped on each side of heel, and one st unwrapped at each end.

Next Row (RS): Knit to last wrapped stitch, k1 (do not lift wrap), w&t next stitch (this stitch will be double wrapped).

Rep last row 19 (27, 35, 43) more times, 1 st rem single wrapped on either side of heel, and 1 unwrapped st at each end.

Foot
Next Rnd: Knit to m (sole sts), sm, work Texture and Cable Pattern Row 7 to end (instep sts).

Dec Rnd: *K1, k2tog, k1; rep from * 9 (11, 13, 15) more times, sm, work Texture and Cable Pattern to end—70 (84, 98, 112) sts.

Next Rnd: Knit to m (sole sts), sm, work Texture and Cable Pattern to end (instep sts).

Cont in patt as est, working sole sts as stockinette and progressing through charted Texture and Cable Pattern for instep sts until foot measures 7¾ (8, 8¼, 8½) in./19.5 (20.5, 21, 21.5) cm from back of heel with heel slightly stretched or 1 (1½, 1¾, 2) in./2.5 (4, 4.5, 5) cm less than desired total length.

Toe
Dec Rnd: Knit to m, sm, *k1, k2tog, k1; rep from * 9 (11, 13, 15) more times—60 (72, 84, 96) sts.

Partial Rnd: Knit to m, remove marker, arrange foll 30 (36, 42, 48) sts onto one needle to work toe.

Short Row 1 (RS): K28 (34, 40, 46), w&t.

Short Row 2 (WS): K26 (32, 38, 44), w&t.

Short Row 3: Knit to 1 st before last wrapped st, w&t.

Rep this last short row 13 (19, 25, 29) more times, 12 (12, 12, 14) sts rem unwrapped in center of work, 8 (11, 14, 16) sts wrapped on each side of heel, and one st unwrapped at each end.

Next Row (RS): Knit to last wrapped st, k1 (do not lift wrap), w&t next st (this st will be double wrapped).

Rep last row 12 (18, 24, 30) more times, 1 st rem single wrapped on either side of heel, and 1 unwrapped st at each end.

Final Row (WS): Knit to m, turn, do not wrap.

Finishing
Cut yarn leaving a 12 in./30.5 cm tail. With tail threaded on a tapestry needle, use the Kitchener Stitch (see Pattern Notes) to graft toe and sole sts. Weave in ends.

Iron Springs Wrap

Worked lengthwise with wide columns of garter stitch interspersed with delicate leaves and vine lace, the Iron Springs Wrap takes texture to another level with crossed sections of mock cables.

For me, a great shawl design has the perfect balance between patterning and simple background stitches like garter stitch. For this shawl, I knew that the patterning would be a strong vertical element in the finished piece and that using a stitch like garter would not only provide a restful area for the eye but also give a horizontal visual to interact with the vertical lace sections. The lace pattern reminds me of tree trunks, deep with the texture of bark and knots, paralleled by reaching vines and rustling leaves.

Explore level/Intermediate: This pattern has very simple patterning on the Adventure Cable such as knits and purls.

Finished Size
66¼ in./168.5 cm long and 17¼ in./44 cm wide over garter stitch, 20 in./51 cm wide over charted section

Yarn
Plymouth Yarn Company Electra Lite (#1 super fine weight; 75% merino wool, 20% nylon, 5% Lurex; 425 yd./388 m per 3.5 oz./100 g): 3 skeins #0008 Bronze

Needles
US size 6 (4.0 mm): 32 in./81 cm circular needle. Adjust needle size if necessary to obtain the correct gauge; circular needle required to accommodate large number of stitches.

Notions
12 markers (m), cable needle (cn) optional, tapestry needle

Gauge
19 sts and 33 rows = 4 in./10 cm in garter stitch, after blocking

Charted Adventure Cables Lace Pattern = 6 in./15 cm

Pattern Notes

This shawl is worked flat back and forth and is cast on for the long edge. To increase or decrease length for this pattern, remove or add an equal number of stitches from the garter stitch sections; please note that this will affect yardage.

Stitch Guide

Garter Stitch
Row 1: Knit.

Rep Row 1 for patt.

Slkyo: Reach right needle tip in front of work and insert into 3rd st from tip, slip 3rd st over first 2 sts from left to right, k1, yo, k1. *See Photo Tutorial on page 40.*

5 stitch increase: [K1, yo, k1, yo, k1] into 1 st.

5 stitch decrease: Sl3 as if to k3tog, k2tog, pass 3 sts over.

Adventure Cables Stitch Guide
With Cable Needle
AC1: 4/4 P1, K3/P1, K3 **RC** with cn: Slip 4 sts to cn and hold in back, p1, k3, and then p1, k3 from cn.

AC2: 4/4 K3, P1/K3, P1 **LC** with cn: Slip 4 sts to cn and hold in front, k3, p1, and then k3, p1 from cn.

Without Cable Needle
AC1: 4/4 P1, K3/P1, K3 **RC** without cn: Reach right needle tip in front of work and insert into the 5th, 6th, 7th, and 8th sts from left tip, slide all 8 sts off left tip, reinsert left tip into first 4 sts in back of work, slide 4 sts from right tip back to left tip, [p1, k3] twice.

AC2: 4/4 K3, P1/K3, P1 **LC** without cn: Reach right needle tip behind work and insert into the 5th, 6th, 7th, and 8th sts from left tip, slide all 8 sts off left tip, reinsert left tip into first 4 sts in front of work, slide 4 sts from right tip back to left tip, [k3, p1] twice.

Iron Springs Wrap Adventure Cables Pattern

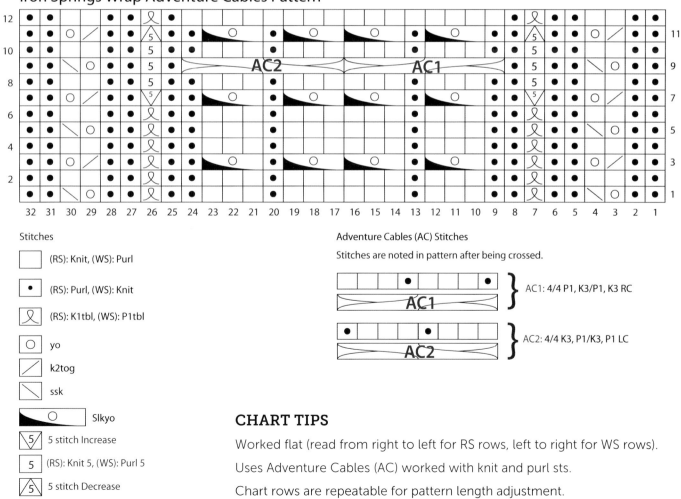

Stitches

☐	(RS): Knit, (WS): Purl
•	(RS): Purl, (WS): Knit
ర	(RS): K1tbl, (WS): P1tbl
○	yo
╱	k2tog
╲	ssk
◼○	Slkyo
5̸	5 stitch Increase
5	(RS): Knit 5, (WS): Purl 5
̸5	5 stitch Decrease

Adventure Cables (AC) Stitches

Stitches are noted in pattern after being crossed.

AC1: 4/4 P1, K3/P1, K3 RC

AC2: 4/4 K3, P1/K3, P1 LC

CHART TIPS

Worked flat (read from right to left for RS rows, left to right for WS rows).

Uses Adventure Cables (AC) worked with knit and purl sts.

Chart rows are repeatable for pattern length adjustment.

INSTRUCTIONS

CO 336 sts using the Old Norwegian method (*see Tutorial below*) or an equally stretchy method of your choice.

Knit 5 rows.

Setup Row (WS): K12, pm, [k32, pm, k24, pm] 5 times, k32, pm, k12.

Pattern Setup Row (RS): [Knit to m, sm, work Adventure Cables Pattern to m, sm] 6 times, knit to end.

Cont in patt as est for 131 more rows, progressing through Rows 2–12 of Adventure Cables Pattern once, and repeating Rows

1–12 of Adventure Cables Pattern 10 more times, working all other stitches in garter stitch.

Border
Knit 5 rows.

BO all sts knitwise on WS row.

Finishing
Wet block shawl to measurements using blocking wires and pins on the vertical edges. On the horizontal sides, allow the lace sections to curve out from the work and the garter sections to curve into the work for a scalloped edge. Weave in ends using a yarn needle.

TUTORIAL: Old Norwegian Cast-on

Leaving a long tail (about 4 times the length of the total needed cast-on), make a slipknot (this counts as the first stitch). Hold the yarn tail around your left thumb and the active yarn end around your index finger with the active yarn in the back. The yarn tail wrapped around the left thumb crosses over itself, creating an "X."

1. Bring the needle underneath the "X" created by the yarn tail wrapped around the thumb, moving the needle away from you and toward the index finger.
2. Bring the needle up behind and then over the furthest loop of the "X," and then down toward you through the space created by the thumb.
3. Bring the needle up over the active yarn and scoop from back to front.

4. Observe the space made by the thumb that the needle just came out of—bring the needle directly back through that space moving the thumb down to untwist the cross, and then drop the loop entirely from the thumb.
5. Bring the thumb underneath the tail to re-cross and tension the yarn.

Rep Steps 1–5 for remaining cast-on stitches.

TUTORIAL: How to Work an Slkyo

The Iron Springs Wrap includes a simple texture stitch called a "slip knit yarn over" (slkyo) that pulls the third stitch on the needle over the first two and then increases a stitch using a yarn over. This technique creates a rounded mock cable that is then crossed over itself in a horseshoe cable pattern. Crossing these vertical lines of mock cables creates an extra layer of texture and depth that gives the Iron Springs Wrap its signature look.

On the chart, the slkyo is depicted over 3 stitches. It begins and ends with 3 stitches, although it increases and decreases a single stitch during the slip and yarn over. The symbol is a swoop depicting the third stitch slipped over the first two, and a yarn over is placed on the center square.

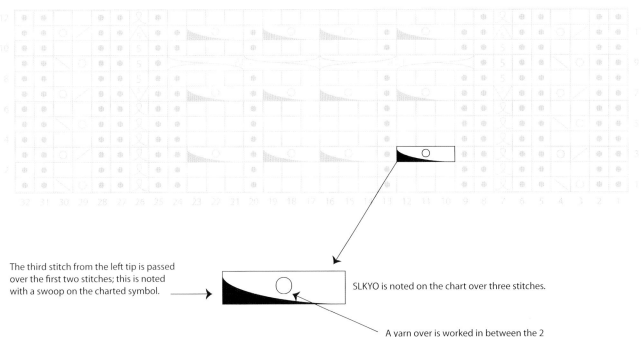

The third stitch from the left tip is passed over the first two stitches; this is noted with a swoop on the charted symbol.

SLKYO is noted on the chart over three stitches.

A yarn over is worked in between the 2 remaining stitches after the pass over.

HOW TO:

1. Work in pattern to the location for the first slkyo.

2. Reach the right needle tip in front of the work and insert into the 3rd st from the left needle tip.

3. Slip this 3rd st over the first 2 sts with the right needle.

4. Drop this st from the right needle; this decreases a st.

5. Knit the 1st st on the left tip.

6. Yarn over 1 st; this increases 1 st.

7. Knit the 2nd st on the left tip.

Kitsap Pullover

Broken rib and twisted knit stitches make for a curve-hugging pullover with unique, textured cables. The Kitsap Pullover is worked flat from the bottom up in pieces with drop sleeves and bound-off shoulder shaping. The wide boatneck is finished simply with a bind-off, as the texture patterns are based on ribbing and lie flat.

I knew that a book on cables needed a deeply cabled pullover, but I also felt that for the textured cables to really pop out, I wanted bands of simple texture. I kept this texture as a twisted rib, and I really love how it keeps the vertical lines of the cables flowing but also gives it a modern horizontal stripe look. This pullover made me think of rocks and fissures when I was knitting it, how the cracks and textures of a cliff seem to move apart and then flow back together creating a surface that at once has individual motifs but also allover consistent texture.

Explore level/Intermediate: This pattern has very simple patterning on the Adventure Cable such as knits and purls.

Finished Sizes
35½ (40½, 44½, 48½, 53) (57, 61, 66, 69½, 73½) in./90 (103, 113, 123, 134.5) (145, 155, 167.5, 176.5, 186.5) cm bust circumference
Shown in size 48½, modeled with 8½ in./21.5 cm of positive ease.

Yarn
Plymouth Yarn Company Worsted Merino Superwash (#4 medium weight; 100% superwash merino wool; 218 yd./199 m per 3.7 oz./100 g): 5 (6, 7, 7, 8) (9, 10, 10, 11, 12) skeins #0001 Natural

Needles
US size 7 (4.5 mm): 32 in./ 81 cm circular or straight needles, 16 in./41 cm circular needles, 1 set of 4 double-pointed needles (dpns). Adjust needle size if necessary to obtain the correct gauge.

Notions
10 removable markers (m), cable needle (cn) optional, tapestry needle

Gauge
20 sts and 28 rows = 4 in./10 cm in stockinette

25¼ sts and 25½ rows = 4 in./10 cm over Adventure Cables Pattern, unstretched

Pattern Notes

This pullover is worked from the bottom up flat in pieces; the seams give this pullover structure and are recommended.

Alteration Information

Note: Any alterations made may affect yardage amounts used.

- ✳ The body length of this garment can easily be adjusted by adding or removing length before the armhole division.
- ✳ Sleeve length can be adjusted by removing or adding rounds worked even before decreases. If a wider cuff is desired, remove decreases in sets of 2 so the cuff rib pattern will still have a multiple of 4 sts in the final count.
- ✳ Upper-arm circumference and armhole depth can be altered by using the sleeve alteration instructions on page 19.

Stitch Guide

Rib Pattern (multiple of 5)
Row 1 (RS): *P1, k1tbl, k1, k1tbl, p1; rep from *.

Row 2 (WS): *K1, p1tbl, k1, p1tbl, k1; rep from *.

Adventure Cables Stitch Guide
With Cable Needle
AC1: 3/1 P1/K1TBL, K1, K1TBL **LC** with cn: Slip 3 sts to cn and hold in front, p1, and then k1tbl, k1, k1tbl from cn.

AC2: 3/1 K1TBL, K1, K1TBL/P1 **RC** with cn: Slip 1 st to cn and hold in back, k1tbl, k1, k1tbl, and then p1 from cn.

AC3: 3/3 K1TBL, K1, K1TBL/K1TBL, K1, K1TBL **LC** with cn: Slip 3 sts to cn and hold in front, k1tbl, k1, k1tbl, and then k1tbl, k1, k1tbl from cn.

AC4: 3/3 K1TBL, K1, K1TBL/K1TBL, K1, K1TBL **RC** with cn: Slip 3 sts to cn and hold in back, k1tbl, k1, k1tbl, and then k1tbl, k1, k1tbl from cn.

Without Cable Needle
AC1: 3/1 P1/K1TBL, K1, K1TBL **LC** without cn: Reach right needle tip behind work and insert into the 4th st from left tip, slide all 4 sts off left tip, reinsert left tip into first 3 sts in front of work, slide 1 st from right tip back to left tip, p1, k1tbl, k1, k1tbl.

AC2 3/1 K1TBL, K1, K1TBL/P1 **RC** without cn: Reach right needle tip in front of work and insert into the 2nd, 3rd, and 4th sts from left tip, slide all 4 sts off left tip, reinsert left tip into 1st st behind work, slide 3 sts from right tip back to left tip, k1tbl, k1, k1tbl, p1.

AC3: 3/3 K1TBL, K1, K1TBL/K1TBL, K1, K1TBL **LC** without cn: Reach right needle tip behind work and insert into the 4th, 5th, and 6th sts from left tip, slide all 6 sts off left tip, reinsert left tip into first 3 sts in front of work, slide 3 sts from right tip back to left tip, [k1tbl, k1, k1tbl] twice.

AC4: 3/3 K1TBL, K1, K1TBL/K1TBL, K1, K1TBL **RC** without cn: Reach right needle tip in front of work and insert into the 4th, 5th, and 6th sts from left tip, slide all 6 sts off left tip, reinsert left tip into first 3 sts behind work, slide 3 sts from right tip back to left tip, [k1tbl, k1, k1tbl] twice.

INSTRUCTIONS

Back

CO 112 (128, 142, 152, 168) (182, 192, 208, 222, 232) sts.

Row 1 (RS): K1, p0 (3, 0, 0, 3) (0, 0, 3, 0, 0), work Rib Pattern to last 1 (4, 1, 1, 4) (1, 1, 4, 1, 1) sts, p0 (3, 0, 0, 3) (0, 0, 3, 0, 0), k1.

Row 2 (WS): K1 (4, 1, 1, 4) (1, 1, 4, 1, 1), work in Rib Pattern to last 1 (4, 1, 1, 4) (1, 1, 4, 1, 1) sts, knit to end.

Cont in patt as est until piece measures 2½ in./6.5 cm from cast-on edge.

Next Row (RS): K1, p5 (3, 0, 5, 3) (0, 5, 3, 0, 5), pm, work Adventure Cables Pattern to last 6 (4, 1, 6, 4) (1, 6, 4, 1, 6) sts, pm, p5 (3, 0, 5, 3) (0, 5, 3, 0, 5), k1.

Next Row (WS): Knit to m, sm, work Adventure Cables Pattern to m, sm, knit to end.

Cont in patt as est working first and last sts as garter, any stitches between single garter st and markers as reverse stockinette and progressing through Rows 2–46, and then repeating Rows 1–46 of Adventure Cables Pattern between markers until piece measures 17 in./43 cm from cast-on edge ending with a WS row.

Place removable markers at the beginning and end of last worked row for sleeve placement.

Cont in patt as est progressing through all patterning until piece measures 5¾ (6, 6½, 7¼, 8¼) (9, 9¾, 10, 10¼, 10¼) in./14.5 (15, 16.5, 18.5, 21) (23, 25, 25.5, 26, 26) cm from marked row ending with a WS row.

During shoulder shaping, discontinue Adventure Cables Chart after completing Row 2, 4, 10, 12, 14, 32, 34, 40, 42, 44, or 46, and then work sts between markers in Rib Pattern for remainder of piece.

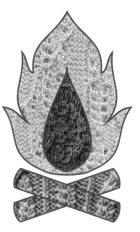

Kitsap Pullover Adventure Cables Pattern

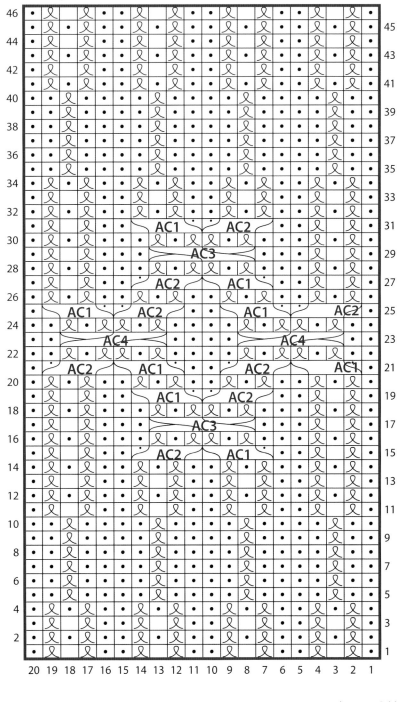

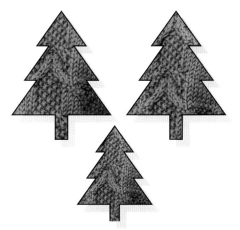

CHART TIPS

Worked flat (read from right to left for RS rows, left to right for WS rows).

Uses Adventure Cables (AC) worked with knit and purl sts.

Entire chart is repeated indicated # of times.

Stitches

☐ (RS): Knit, (WS): Purl

• (RS): Purl, (WS): Knit

Ω (RS): K1tbl (WS): P1tbl

Borders

— Stitch Repeat

Adventure Cables (AC) Stitches
Stitches are noted in pattern after being crossed.

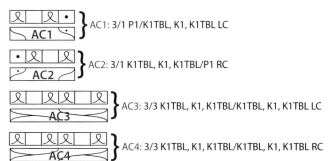

AC1: 3/1 P1/K1TBL, K1, K1TBL LC

AC2: 3/1 K1TBL, K1, K1TBL/P1 RC

AC3: 3/3 K1TBL, K1, K1TBL/K1TBL, K1, K1TBL LC

AC4: 3/3 K1TBL, K1, K1TBL/K1TBL, K1, K1TBL RC

Shoulder Shaping

BO 6 (5, 7, 8, 8) (9, 10, 11, 10, 11) sts at beg of next 6 (8, 8, 8, 10) (10, 10, 10, 12, 12) rows—76 (88, 86, 88, 88) (92, 92, 98, 102, 100) sts.

BO 7 (13, 11, 12, 11) (12, 11, 14, 16, 15) at beg of foll 2 rows—62 (62, 64, 64, 66) (68, 70, 70, 70, 70) sts.

BO rem sts, placing removable marker at beg and end of bound-off row.

Front

Work same as Back.

Seaming

Using tapestry needle seam front to back from hem to marked row up each side of pullover. Seam shoulder from armhole edge to marked stitch from bind-off row.

Sleeves

Using 16 in./41 cm circular needle, pick up and knit 58 (60, 66, 72, 82) (90, 98, 100, 102, 102) sts evenly around armhole opening, join to work in the round, and pm (place marker) for beg of rnd.

Knit 11 (11, 7, 6, 3) (2, 2, 2, 2, 2) rnds even.

Dec Rnd: K1, k2tog, knit to last 3 sts, ssk, k1—2 sts decreased.

Rep Dec Rnd every 12 (12, 8, 7, 4) (3, 3, 3, 3, 3) rnds 5 (5, 8, 10, 14) (17, 20, 20, 20, 20) more times—46 (48, 48, 50, 52) (54, 56, 58, 60, 60) sts.

Take a minute to try on the sweater at this point to see how the sleeve fits before continuing to add extra length. You may want to skip straight to the cuff.

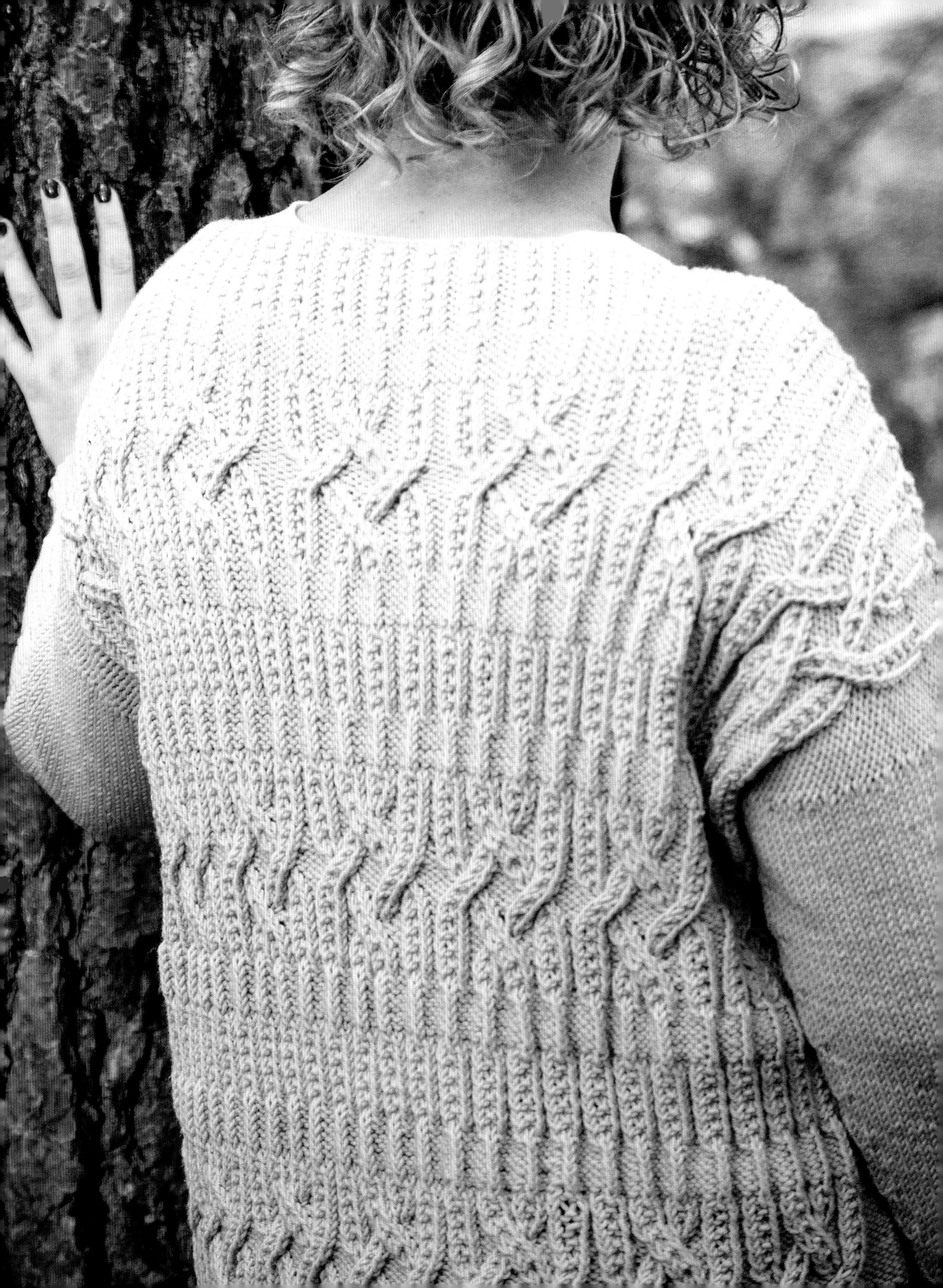

Work even to 12¾ (12¾, 12¾, 12½, 11½) (10¾, 10½, 10½, 10½, 10¼) in./32.5 (32.5, 32.5, 32, 29) (27.5, 26.5, 26.5, 26.5, 26) cm or until 2½ in./6.5 cm shorter than desired sleeve length.

Next Rnd: *K1tbl, p1; rep from * to end of rnd.

Rep last rnd for an additional 2½ in./6.5 cm. BO all sts in patt.

Finishing
Work in any loose ends using tapestry needle.

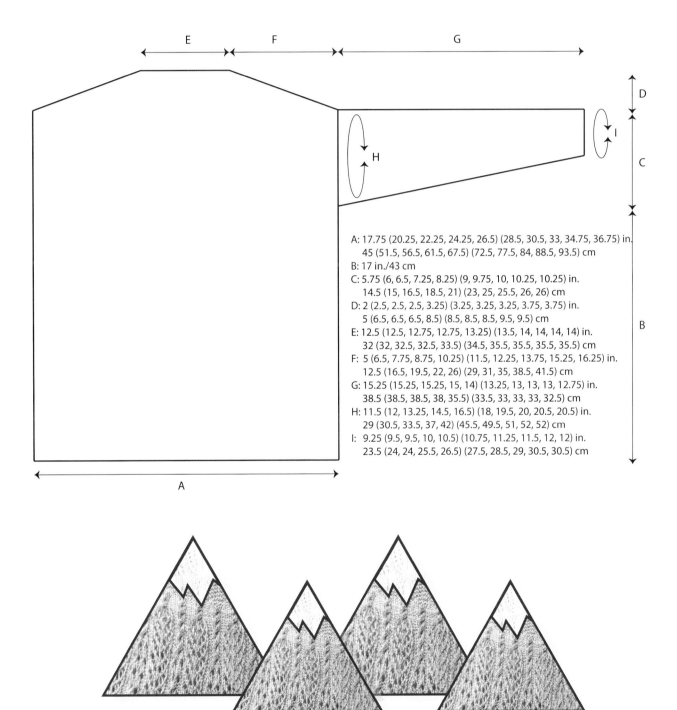

A: 17.75 (20.25, 22.25, 24.25, 26.5) (28.5, 30.5, 33, 34.75, 36.75) in. 45 (51.5, 56.5, 61.5, 67.5) (72.5, 77.5, 84, 88.5, 93.5) cm
B: 17 in./43 cm
C: 5.75 (6, 6.5, 7.25, 8.25) (9, 9.75, 10, 10.25, 10.25) in. 14.5 (15, 16.5, 18.5, 21) (23, 25, 25.5, 26, 26) cm
D: 2 (2.5, 2.5, 2.5, 3.25) (3.25, 3.25, 3.25, 3.75, 3.75) in. 5 (6.5, 6.5, 6.5, 8.5) (8.5, 8.5, 8.5, 9.5, 9.5) cm
E: 12.5 (12.5, 12.75, 12.75, 13.25) (13.5, 14, 14, 14, 14) in. 32 (32, 32.5, 32.5, 33.5) (34.5, 35.5, 35.5, 35.5, 35.5) cm
F: 5 (6.5, 7.75, 8.75, 10.25) (11.5, 12.25, 13.75, 15.25, 16.25) in. 12.5 (16.5, 19.5, 22, 26) (29, 31, 35, 38.5, 41.5) cm
G: 15.25 (15.25, 15.25, 15, 14) (13.25, 13, 13, 13, 12.75) in. 38.5 (38.5, 38.5, 38, 35.5) (33.5, 33, 33, 33, 32.5) cm
H: 11.5 (12, 13.25, 14.5, 16.5) (18, 19.5, 20, 20.5, 20.5) in. 29 (30.5, 33.5, 37, 42) (45.5, 49.5, 51, 52, 52) cm
I: 9.25 (9.5, 9.5, 10, 10.5) (10.75, 11.25, 11.5, 12, 12) in. 23.5 (24, 24, 25.5, 26.5) (27.5, 28.5, 29, 30.5, 30.5) cm

Thavis Shrug

Worked from the bottom up, this textured cocoon-style shrug has a wide front border of textured Adventure Cables and short-row dolman sleeves. The back neck has a narrow band of seed stitches seamed at the top of the point and a border of seed stitches up the top of the sleeves and at the hem.

I wanted to really play with seed stitch texture for this shrug and used the purl stitch as a graphic texture in the V shapes as well as moving knit stitches over seed stitches for a subtly textured cable pattern. So many times we see cables as a really strong graphic image, but in this stitch pattern I wanted the cables to enhance the texture and create surface interest rather than steal the show. This pattern will always remind me of evergreen trees, the subtle shifting textures and patterns of needles overlapped, creating a single tree of many individual branches.

Explore level/Intermediate: This pattern has very simple patterning on the Adventure Cable such as knits and purls.

Finished Sizes

32 (39¾, 48, 55¾, 64, 71¾) in./81.5 (101, 122, 141.5, 162.5, 182) cm bust circumference

Shown in size 48, modeled with 8½ in./21.5 cm of positive ease.

Yarn

Berroco Yarn Ultra Wool Worsted (#4 medium weight, 100% wool; 219 yd./200 m per 3.5 oz./100 g): 4 (5, 6, 7, 8, 9) skeins #3340 Arbor

Needles

US sizes 6 (4.0 mm) and 7 (4.5 mm): 32 in./81 cm circular; a circular needle is required to accommodate the large number of stitches for the sleeves. Adjust needle size if necessary to obtain the correct gauge.

Notions

2 stitch markers (m), 2 removable stitch markers, cable needle (cn) optional, tapestry needle, stitch holder or waste yarn

Gauge

18 sts and 24 rows = 4 in./10 cm in stockinette

37 sts = 7½ in./19 cm over Adventure Cables Pattern, lightly steam blocked

Pattern Notes

This shrug is worked from the bottom up with dolman-style sleeves cast on and worked at the same time as the main body. The tops of the sleeves and the shoulders are shaped with short rows, and the final few rows at the top of the sleeves are worked with seed stitch. Seaming the top and bottom edges of the sleeves is recommended for stability in the garment. The Adventure Cables patterning in this chart uses knit stitches and purl stitches, continuing the seed stitch pattern during the cable crossings.

During short-row shaping continue Adventure Cables patterning as much as possible; 37 sts used for Adventure Cables are worked in seed stitch during final short rows.

Stitch Guide

Seed Stitch (multiple of 2 sts plus 1)
Row 1 (RS): *K1, p1; rep from * to 1 st before end (or marker), k1.

Rep Row 1 for patt.

w&t (wrap and turn): Bring yarn between needles to *opposite side* of work, slip next st to right tip, bring yarn between needles to *opposite side* of work, slip st back to left tip, turn work.

Adventure Cables Stitch Guide
With Cable Needle
AC1: 2/3 K2/P1, K1, P1 RC with cn: Slip 3 sts to cn and hold in back, k2, and then p1, k1, p1 from cn.

AC2: 2/3 P1, K1, P1/K2 LC with cn: Slip 2 sts to cn and hold in front, p1, k1, p1, and then k2 from cn.

AC3: 3/2 P1, K1, P1/K2 RC with cn: Slip 2 sts to cn and hold in back, p1, k1, p1, and then k2 from cn.

AC4: 3/2 K2/P1, K1, P1 LC with cn: Slip 3 sts to cn and hold in front, k2, and then p1, k1, p1 from cn.

Without Cable Needle
AC1: 2/3 K2/P1, K1, P1 RC without cn: Reach right needle tip in front of work and insert into the 4th and 5th sts from left tip, slide all 5 sts off left tip, reinsert left tip into first 3 sts behind work, slide 2 sts from right tip back to left tip, k2, p1, k1, p1.

AC2: 2/3 P1, K1, P1/K2 LC without cn: Reach right needle tip behind work and insert into the 3rd, 4th, and 5th sts from left tip, slide all 5 sts off left tip, reinsert left tip into first 2 sts in front of work, slide 3 sts from right tip back to left tip, p1, k1, p1, k2.

AC3: 3/2 P1, K1, P1/K2 RC without cn: Reach right needle tip in front of work and insert into the 3rd, 4th, and 5th sts from left tip, slide all 5 sts off left tip, reinsert left tip into first 2 sts behind work, slide 3 sts from right tip back to left tip, p1, k1, p1, k2.

AC4: 3/2 K2/P1, K1, P1 LC without cn: Reach right needle tip behind work and insert into the 4th and 5th sts from left tip, slide all 5 sts off left tip, reinsert left tip into first 3 sts in front of work, slide 2 sts from right tip back to left tip, k2, p1, k1, p1.

INSTRUCTIONS

Back

Using smaller needles, CO 73 (91, 109, 127, 145, 163) sts.

Work seed stitch over all sts until piece measures 1¾ in./4.5 cm from cast-on edge. End with WS row.

Change to larger needles.

Next Row (RS): Knit to end.

Next Row (WS): K1, purl to last st, k1.

Cont in patt as est, working first and last sts as garter and all other sts as stockinette, until piece measures 14½ (14, 13½, 13, 12¾, 12¼) in./37 (35.5, 34.5, 33, 32.5, 31) cm from cast-on edge. End with WS row.

Sleeve Shaping

Next Row (RS): CO 48 sts using the Backward Loop Method, work first 9 sts in seed stitch, pm, knit to end—121 (139, 157, 175, 193, 211) sts.

Next Row (WS): CO 48 sts using the Backward Loop Method, work first 9 sts in seed stitch, pm, knit to m, sm, work seed stitch to end—169 (187, 205, 223, 241, 259) sts.

Thavis Shrug Adventure Cables Pattern

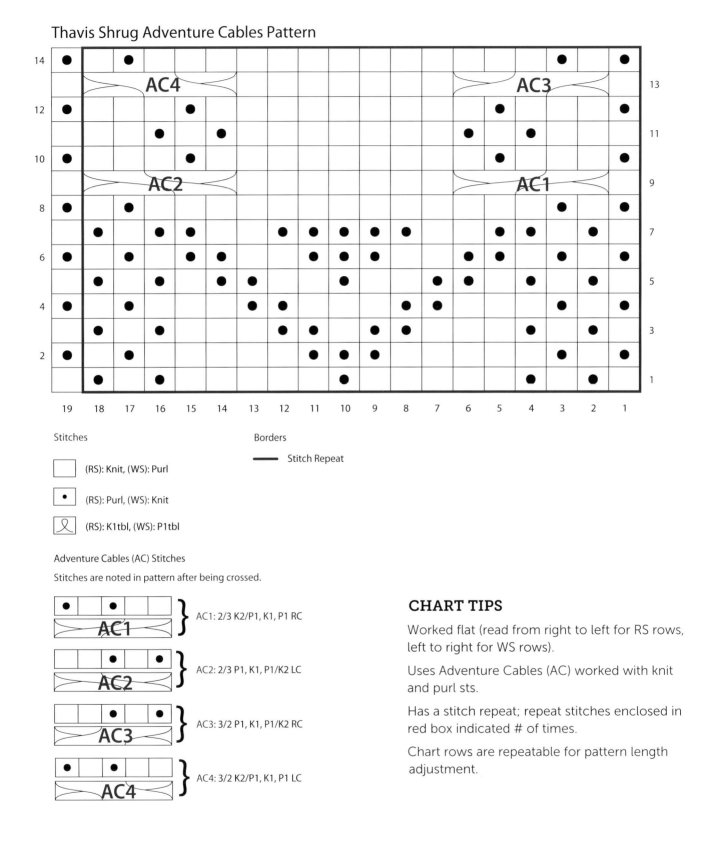

Stitches

☐ (RS): Knit, (WS): Purl

• (RS): Purl, (WS): Knit

⟨ (RS): K1tbl, (WS): P1tbl

Borders

— Stitch Repeat

Adventure Cables (AC) Stitches

Stitches are noted in pattern after being crossed.

AC1: 2/3 K2/P1, K1, P1 RC

AC2: 2/3 P1, K1, P1/K2 LC

AC3: 3/2 P1, K1, P1/K2 RC

AC4: 3/2 K2/P1, K1, P1 LC

CHART TIPS

Worked flat (read from right to left for RS rows, left to right for WS rows).

Uses Adventure Cables (AC) worked with knit and purl sts.

Has a stitch repeat; repeat stitches enclosed in red box indicated # of times.

Chart rows are repeatable for pattern length adjustment.

Cont in patt as est, working first and last 9 sts in seed stitch and all other sts in stockinette, until piece measures 4¼ (4¾, 5¼, 5½, 6, 6½) in./11 (12, 13.5, 14, 15, 16.5) cm from sleeve cast-on, ending with a WS row.

Short Rows
Short Row 1 (RS): Work to last 4 sts, w&t.

Short Row 2 (WS): Work to last 4 sts, w&t.

Short Row 3: Work to 4 sts before last wrapped st, w&t.

Rep this last short row 33 (37, 43, 47, 51, 55) more times; there are 18 (20, 23, 25, 27, 29) wrapped sts on each side of the work, 36 (40, 46, 50, 54, 58) wraps total.

Next Row (RS): Knit to m working in wraps, sm, work seed stitch to end working in wraps.

Next Row (WS): Work seed stitch to m, sm, purl to m working in wraps, sm, work seed stitch to end working in wraps.

Change to smaller needles; work seed stitch over all sts for 3 rows.

Final Row (WS): BO 84 (93, 102, 111, 120, 129) sts in patt, place removable m into edge of work, BO 1, place removable m into edge of work, BO rem 84 (93, 102, 111, 120, 129) sts in patt.

Left Front

Using smaller needles CO 41 (49, 59, 67, 77, 85) sts.

Work seed stitch over all sts until piece measures 1¾ in./4.5 cm from cast-on edge.

Change to larger needles.

Pattern Setup Row (RS): K4 (12, 22, 30, 40, 48), pm, work Adventure Cables Chart over rem 37 sts, working sts in marked box twice total.

Next Row (WS): Work Adventure Cables Pattern to m, sm, purl to last st, k1.

Cont in patt as est, progressing through Rows 3–14 of Adventure Cables Chart once and repeating Rows 1–14, working 1st st as a garter stitch and all other sts as stockinette until piece measures 14½ (14, 13½, 13, 12¾, 12¼) in./37 (35.5, 34.5, 33, 32.5, 31) cm from cast-on edge, ending with a WS row.

Sleeve Shaping

Next Row (RS): CO 48 sts using the Backward Loop Method, work first 9 sts in seed stitch, pm, knit to m, sm, work Adventure Cables Chart to end—89 (97, 107, 115, 125, 133) sts.

Next Row (WS): Work Adventure Cables Chart to m, sm, purl to m, work seed stitch to end.

Cont in patt as est, working first 9 sts in seed stitch, progressing in Adventure Cables Pattern, and working all other sts in stockinette, until piece measures 4¼ (4¾, 5¼, 5½, 6, 6½) in./11 (12, 13.5, 14, 15, 16.5) cm from cast-on edge, ending with a RS row.

Short Rows

Short Row 1 (WS): Work to last 4 sts, w&t.

Short Row 2 (RS): Work to end.

Short Row 3: Work to 4 sts before last wrapped st, w&t.

Short Row 4: Work to end.

Rep these last two short rows 16 (18, 21, 23, 25, 27) more times; there are 18 (20, 23, 25, 27, 29) wraps total.

Next Row (WS): Work seed stitch to m working in wraps, sm, purl to m working in wraps, sm, work seed stitch to end working in wraps.

Change to smaller needles, work seed stitch over all sts for 3 rows.

Final Row (WS): Work 5 (4, 5, 4, 5) sts in patt, place onto holder or waste yarn, BO rem sts in patt.

Right Front
Using smaller needles CO 41 (49, 59, 67, 77, 85) sts.

Work seed stitch over all sts until piece measures 1¾ in./4.5 cm from cast-on edge.

Change to larger needles.

Pattern Setup Row (RS): Work Adventure Cables Chart over first 37 sts, working sts in marked box twice total, pm, k4 (12, 22, 30, 40, 48).

Next Row (WS): K1, purl to m, sm, work Adventure Cables Chart to end.

Cont in patt as est, progressing through Rows 3–14 of Adventure Cables Chart once and repeating Rows 1–14, working 1st st as a garter stitch and all other sts as stockinette until piece measures 14½ (14, 13½, 13, 12¾, 12¼) in./37 (35.5, 34.5, 33, 32.5, 31) cm from cast-on edge, ending with a RS row.

Sleeve Shaping
Next Row (WS): CO 48 sts using the Backward Loop Method, work first 9 sts in seed stitch, pm, purl to m, sm, work Adventure Cables Chart to end—89 (97, 107, 115, 125, 133) sts.

Next Row (RS): Work Adventure Cables Chart to m, sm, knit to m, work seed stitch to end.

Cont in patt as est, working last 9 sts in seed stitch, progressing in Adventure Cables Pattern, and working all other sts in stockinette, until piece measures 4¼ (4¾, 5¼, 5½, 6½) in./11 (12, 13.5, 14, 15, 16.5) cm from cast-on edge, ending with a WS row.

Short Rows
Short Row 1 (RS): Work to last 4 sts, w&t.

Short Row 2 (WS): Work to end.

Short Row 3: Work to 4 sts before last wrapped st, w&t.

Short Row 4: Work to end.

Rep these last two short rows 16 (18, 21, 23, 25, 27) more times; there are 18 (20, 23, 25, 27, 29) wraps total.

Next Row (RS): Work seed stitch to m working in wraps, sm, purl to m working in wraps, sm, work seed stitch to end working in wraps.

Next Row (WS): Work seed stitch to m, sm, purl to m, sm, work seed stitch to end.

Change to smaller needles, work seed stitch over all sts for 3 rows.

Final Row (WS): BO 84 (93, 102, 111, 120, 129) sts, place rem 5 (4, 5, 4, 5, 4) sts onto holder or waste yarn, cut yarn leaving 10 in./25.5 cm tail for seaming.

Finishing
Using tapestry needle, seam fronts to back from hem up side and under sleeve. Seam tops of sleeves from cuff to marked st at center back, seam held sts together, and then seam to single stitch at center back. Work in any loose ends, steam block lightly to set patt.

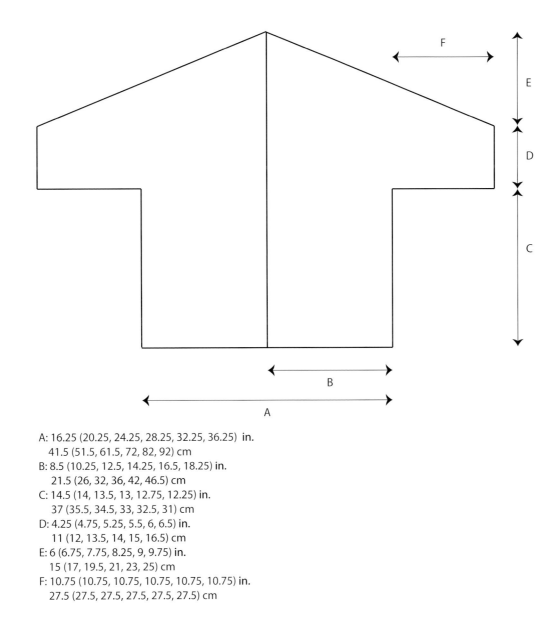

A: 16.25 (20.25, 24.25, 28.25, 32.25, 36.25) in.
   41.5 (51.5, 61.5, 72, 82, 92) cm
B: 8.5 (10.25, 12.5, 14.25, 16.5, 18.25) in.
   21.5 (26, 32, 36, 42, 46.5) cm
C: 14.5 (14, 13.5, 13, 12.75, 12.25) in.
   37 (35.5, 34.5, 33, 32.5, 31) cm
D: 4.25 (4.75, 5.25, 5.5, 6, 6.5) in.
   11 (12, 13.5, 14, 15, 16.5) cm
E: 6 (6.75, 7.75, 8.25, 9, 9.75) in.
   15 (17, 19.5, 21, 23, 25) cm
F: 10.75 (10.75, 10.75, 10.75, 10.75, 10.75) in.
   27.5 (27.5, 27.5, 27.5, 27.5, 27.5) cm

CHAPTER

LACE

CROSSINGS

CROSSINGS WITH

LACE STITCHES

Lace stitches are a study of holes and how to artfully arrange them within a knitted fabric to make patterns and shapes. Most of these holes are created with a simple yarn over combined with a left- or right-leaning decrease. The projects in this chapter primarily deal with vertical sections of lace patterning that are then moved across each other. Since lace patterning is mainly composed of negative space (the holes), the challenge was to cross these holes over each other and still have the patterning be read as a pattern while potentially blocking the hole with crossed stitches on the back side. The solution was to arrange the lace patterning in vertical columns, many times with a section of purl stitches on either side to accentuate the patterning. Pomona Shawl, Odessa Tee, and Bainbridge Wrap are three forays into vertical sections of lace stitches crossed over one another, while Palouse Falls Shawl has a single twisted knit stitch crossed over areas of simple lace.

WHAT TO EXPECT

The "Crossings with Lace Stitches" projects include vertical lace patterns worked with a combination of increases and decreases that are then moved across the background. Stitches include but are not limited to knit, purl, yarn over, ssk, k2tog, and cdd. The ability to work simple lace patterns and cross cables is required for this chapter.

SKILL LEVELS INCLUDED

"Crossings with Lace Stitches" includes one Explore level pattern and three Adventure level patterns.

Pomona Shawl

Worked lengthwise from the bottom up with sections of geometric lace and lace Adventure Cables, the Pomona Shawl starts with a bang and finishes with simple garter stitch. The combination of decreasing stitches and working crossed stitches shapes the lower lace section while the garter stitch section contains short rows to create a beautiful crescent shape. The pattern calls for a light fingering weight, but a larger yarn could easily be used for a larger shawl (keep in mind that this change will affect yardage). The cables in this shawl move sections of lace stitches but do not have any lace worked over the cable crossing.

I especially love to work shawls from the bottom up since I find that my enthusiasm for the project is strongest at the beginning, making the longest rows go faster, and when my attention span is waning, the rows are shorter and (in this case) simpler. The stitch pattern for this shawl was a very organic process to design. When working the swatch I had the two vertical sections of lace planned out, but the decreases and the placement of the top cables were very intuitive and not planned beforehand at all. The stitch pattern reminds me of water reeds and the lakeshore, the flickering reflections off the water surface as it dances among the vertical plant stalks.

Explore level/Intermediate: This pattern has very simple patterning on the Adventure Cable such as knits and purls.

Finished Size
46 in./117 cm wide and 13¾ in./35 cm tall at the ends and 17½ in./44.5 cm tall at center

Yarn
Valley Yarns Charlemont (#1 super fine weight; 60% merino wool, 20% silk, 20% nylon; 439 yd./401 m per 3.5 oz./100 g): 2 skeins Light Grey (the sample used 4.2 oz./ 120 g [522 yd./477 m] exactly)

Needles
US size 6 (4.0 mm): 32 in./81 cm circular needle. Adjust needle size if necessary to obtain the correct gauge; circular needle required to accommodate large number of stitches.

Notions
Cable needle (cn) optional, tapestry needle

Gauge
15½ sts and 36 rows = 4 in./10 cm in garter stitch after blocking

18 sts and 23½ rows = 4 in./10 cm over Lace Pattern after blocking

Pattern Notes

This shawl is worked flat back and forth; the cast-on is the bottom edge of the lace. It is essential to use a stretchy cast-on for this shawl so that the bottom edge can be pinned into a scalloped edge when blocking. It is not necessary to lift the short row wraps in the garter stitch section—simply work across the wrapped stitches, and they will blend into the garter stitch.

Alteration Information

Note: *Any alterations made may affect yardage amounts used.*

✳ Additional repeats of the Chart A Rows 1–16 can be worked to increase length; end any added repeats on a Row 16.
✳ Charts B and C *cannot* be repeated to increase size.

✳ Stitches can be added to the cast-on in 40 st increments to increase width. If you choose to increase the cast-on, you need to add 20 sts to Short Row 1 for every repeat of the charted pattern added to the cast-on. Repeat Short Row 3 eight more times for each repeat of the charted pattern added to the cast-on.
✳ Additional garter stitch rows can be added after the short rows are complete.

Stitch Guide

Garter Stitch
Row 1: Knit.

Rep Row 1 for patt.

w&t (wrap and turn): Bring yarn between needles to *opposite side* of work, slip next st to right tip, bring yarn between needles to *opposite side* of work, slip st back to left tip, turn work.

With Cable Needle
3/1/3 K3/P1/K3 RC: Slip 4 sts to cn and hold in back, k3, sl last st from cn to left tip, p1, sl 3 rem sts from cn to left tip, k3.

3/3 RC: Slip 3 sts to cn and hold in back, k3, k3 from cn.

Without Cable Needle
3/1/3 K3/P1/K3 RC: Reach right tip in front of work and insert into the 5th, 6th, and 7th sts from left tip, slide 7 sts off left tip, reinsert left tip into first 4 sts behind work, slide 3 sts from right tip to left tip, k3. Reach right tip in front of work and insert into 4th st from tip, slide 4 sts off left tip, reinsert left tip into 3 sts behind work, slide 1 st from right tip to left tip, p1, k3.

3/3 RC: Reach right tip in front of work and insert into the 4th, 5th, and 6th sts from left tip, slide 6 sts off left tip, reinsert left tip into first 3 sts behind work, slide 3 sts from right tip to left tip, k6.

Knitted Cast-on: Create one stitch using a slipknot, insert needle as if to knit, *wrap and pull through, place made stitch onto left needle twisting needle clockwise (stitch is placed onto left tip with right leg of stitch forward, right tip should be inserted into stitch that is being slipped so as to immediately knit stitch again); rep from * for remainder of cast-on.

INSTRUCTIONS

CO 293 sts using the knitted cast-on or stretchy method of your choice.

Knit 2 rows.

Lace Section
Chart A
Setup Row (RS): K3, pm, work Chart A to last 3 sts working marked repeat (sts 1–40) a total of 7 times, and working sts 41–47 once, pm, k3.

Cont in patt as est for 47 more rows, progressing through Rows 2–16 of Chart A once, and repeating 1–16 of Chart A 2 more times, working edge sts in garter stitch as established.

Chart B

Next Row (RS): K3, sm, work Chart B to last 3 sts working marked repeat (sts 1–19) a total of 14 times, and working sts 20–25 once, sm, k3—278 sts.

Cont in patt as est for 13 more rows, progressing through Rows 2–14 of Chart B once—236 sts.

Chart C

Next Row (RS): K3, sm, work Chart C to last 3 sts working marked repeat (sts 1–8) a total of 28 times, and working sts 9–14 once, sm, k3.

Cont in patt as est for 7 more rows, progressing through Rows 2–8 of Lace Chart C once—178 sts.

Garter Section

Short Row 1 (RS): K93, w&t.

Short Row 2 (WS): K8, w&t.

Short Row 3: Knit to wrap, knit wrapped stitch (do not lift wrap), k4, w&t.

Rep this last short row 31 more times, 4 sts rem unworked on each side.

Next Row (RS): Knit to end.

Next Row (WS): Knit to end.

Cont in garter stitch over all sts for 11 more rows, loosely BO all sts knitwise on the WS.

Finishing

Wet block shawl to measurements using blocking wires and pins. Weave in ends using a yarn needle.

Pomona Shawl Chart A

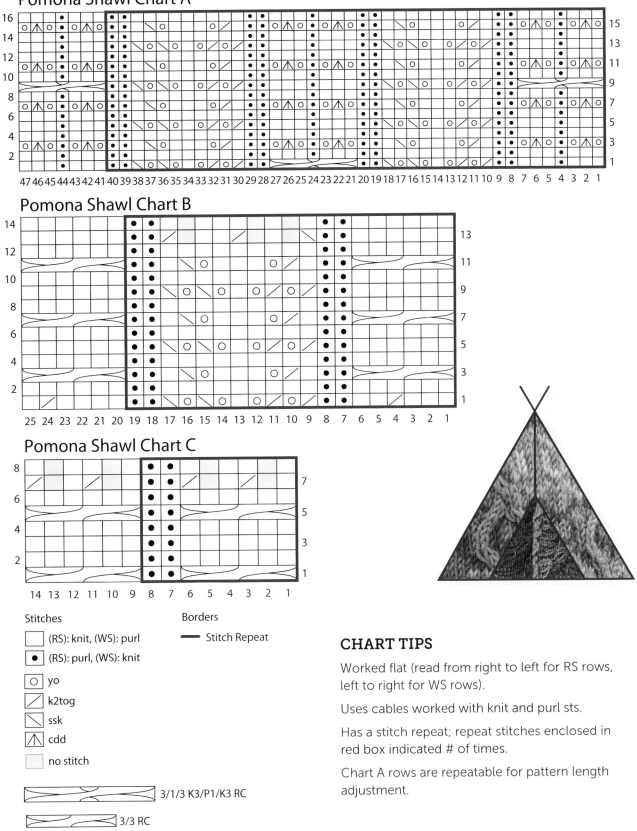

Pomona Shawl Chart B

Pomona Shawl Chart C

Stitches

	(RS): knit, (WS): purl
●	(RS): purl, (WS): knit
O	yo
╱	k2tog
╲	ssk
⋀	cdd
	no stitch

3/1/3 K3/P1/K3 RC

3/3 RC

Borders

— Stitch Repeat

CHART TIPS

Worked flat (read from right to left for RS rows, left to right for WS rows).

Uses cables worked with knit and purl sts.

Has a stitch repeat; repeat stitches enclosed in red box indicated # of times.

Chart A rows are repeatable for pattern length adjustment.

Odessa Tee

Worked flat from the bottom up in pieces, this T-shirt is seamed to add structure in the flowing yarn and lace stitch pattern. Bands of texture and lace loop over each other in beautiful swooping Adventure Cables that create a dramatic allover pattern. The wide neck and dolman sleeves on this pullover tee have simple shaping for a striking silhouette that allows the stitch pattern to really shine.

Since we are at adventure camp, it seemed like a T-shirt was an inevitable addition, but the goal was to make a T-shirt *worthy* of the gorgeous human I was designing it for—that's you! I really wanted to emphasize the lace inside the crossing stitches in this stitch motif, and so I chose very linear patterns that visually read as vertical columns. One column is a vertical eyelet pattern all the way up, while the other is similar but different, creating thick-and-thin movement in the columns. The patterning will always remind me of gently curling smoke tendrils from a barely burning fire that twist over and around each other into the air.

Adventure level/Advanced Intermediate: This pattern has moderate patterning on the Adventure Cable such as increases, decreases, or slipped stitches.

Finished Sizes
42 (52½, 63, 73½, 84) in./106.5 (133.5, 160, 186.5, 213.5) cm bust circumference
    Shown in size 42, modeled with 1 in./2.5 cm of positive ease.

Yarn
Plymouth Yarn Company R.S.S. Reserve Sport Solid (#4 medium weight; 45% extra fine merino wool, 35% mulberry silk, 20% bamboo; 348 yd./318 m per 3.5 oz./100 g): 3 (4, 6, 7, 7) skeins #0001 Naturale

Needles
US sizes 6 (4.0 mm) and 7 (4.5 mm): 32 in./81 cm circular, and size 6 (4.0 mm) 24 in./61 cm circular and double-pointed needles (dpns). A circular needle is required to accommodate the large number of stitches for the sleeves. Adjust needle size if necessary to obtain the correct gauge.

Notions
2 removable stitch markers, cable needle (cn) optional, tapestry needle

Gauge
20¾ sts and 25½ rows = 4 in./10 cm over Adventure Cables Pattern, after wet blocking and drying

One repeat of 28 sts = 5¼ in./13.5 cm, after blocking and drying

17 sts = 4 in./10 cm over garter stitch (for hem, collar, and cuffs)

Pattern Notes

This tee is worked in two pieces from the bottom up. The sleeves are created by casting on stitches to either side of the lower body and working them at the same time as the front or back respectively. The front and back are seamed to each other at the sides, under-arms, and shoulders. It is essential to wet block your swatches to determine gauge and wet block the final piece to set the pattern. When measuring the length of this pattern for the lower body and the sleeve depth, take note of the suggested number of rows to work—this pattern can stretch when blocked, creating a longer garment. The sample shown stretched 3 in./7.6 cm between the knitting and the blocking. It is important to note that the measurements provided are for a sample that is wet blocked, dried, and then left to relax for at least 24 hours.

Alteration Information

Note: *Any alterations made may affect yard-age amounts used.*

* The body length of this garment can easily be adjusted by adding or removing length before the sleeve shaping.
* If altering the length of the lower body or armholes OR if your stated row gauge does not match the pattern, you can calculate needed rows as follows: Take the total rows worked on a wet blocked and dried swatch and divide it by the total length worked of the wet blocked and dried swatch—this equals

your rows per inch. Multiply this number by your needed length = total rows in pattern to work.

* If you are adding rows to lengthen the armhole, add these rows to the first "work even" section of the armhole. This will allow the collar to still work with the neck shaping.

* Each size up in this pattern is an additional repeat of the chart on the back and front of the shirt. If you need to adjust the circumference, try working the pattern with a smaller or larger needle.

* A-line shaping can be achieved by using a larger needle for the cast-on and half the lower body, and a smaller needle for the remainder of the garment.

Adventure Cables Stitch Guide
With Cable Needle

AC1: 5/1 P1/P2, K1TBL, P2 **LC** with cn: Slip 5 sts to cn and hold in front, p1, and then p2, k1tbl, p2 from cn.

AC2: 5/1 K2TOG, YO, K1, YO, SSK/P1 **RC** with cn: Slip 1 st to cn and hold in back, k2tog, yo, k1, yo, ssk, and then p1 from cn.

AC3: 5/5 K2TOG, YO, K1, YO, SSK/P2, K1TBL, P2 **RC** with cn: Slip 5 sts to cn and hold in back, k2tog, yo, k1, yo, ssk, and then p2, k1tbl, p2 from cn.

AC4: 5/1 P1/K2TOG, YO, K1, YO, SSK **LC** with cn: Slip 5 sts to cn and hold in front, p1, and then k2tog, yo, k1, yo, ssk from cn.

AC5: 5/1 P2, K1TBL, P2/P1 **RC** with cn: Slip 1 st to cn and hold in back, p2, k1tbl, p2, and then p1 from cn.

AC6: 5/5 P2, K1TBL, P2/K2TOG, YO, K1, YO, SSK **RC** with cn: Slip 5 sts to cn and hold in back, p2, k1tbl, p2, and then k2tog, yo, k1, yo, ssk from cn.

Without Cable Needle

AC1: 5/1 P1/P2, K1TBL, P2 **LC** without cn: Reach right needle tip behind work and insert into the 6th stitch from left tip, slide all 6 sts off left tip, reinsert left tip into first 5 sts in front of work, slide 1 st from right tip back to left tip, p1, p2, k1tbl, p2.

AC2: 5/1 K2TOG, YO, K1, YO, SSK/P1 **RC** without cn: Reach right needle tip in front of work and insert into the 2nd, 3rd, 4th, 5th, and 6th sts from left tip, slide all 6 sts off left tip, reinsert left tip into first st behind work, slide 5 sts from right tip back to left tip, k2tog, yo, k1, yo, ssk, p1.

AC3: 5/5 K2TOG, YO, K1, YO, SSK/P2, K1TBL, P2 **RC** without cn: Reach right needle tip in front of work and insert into the 6th, 7th, 8th, 9th, and 10th sts from left tip, slide all 10 sts off left tip, reinsert left tip into first 5 sts behind work, slide 5 sts from right tip back to left tip, k2tog, yo, k1, yo, ssk, p2, k1tbl, p2.

AC4: 5/1 P1/K2TOG, YO, K1, YO, SSK **LC** without cn: Reach right needle tip behind work and insert into the 6th st from left tip, slide all 6 sts off left tip, reinsert left tip into first 5 sts in front of work, slide 1 st from right tip back to left tip, p1, k2tog, yo, k1, yo, ssk.

AC5: 5/1 P2, K1TBL, P2/P1 **RC** without cn: Reach right needle tip in front of work and insert into the 2nd, 3rd, 4th, 5th, and 6th sts from left tip, slide all 6 sts off left tip, reinsert left tip into first st behind work, slide 5 sts from right tip back to left tip, p2, k1tbl, p2, p1.

AC6: 5/5 P2, K1TBL, P2/K2TOG, YO, K1, YO, SSK **RC** without cn: Reach right needle tip in front of work and insert into the 6th, 7th, 8th, 9th, and 10th sts from left tip, slide all 10 sts off left tip, reinsert left tip into first 5 sts behind work, slide 5 sts from right tip back to left tip, p2, k1tbl, p2, k2tog, yo, k1, yo, ssk.

INSTRUCTIONS

Back
Using smaller 32 in./81 cm circular needle, CO 114 (142, 170, 198, 226) sts.

Knit 4 rows.

Change to larger 32 in./81 cm circular needle.

Next Row (RS): K1, p1, *k5, p2; rep from * to last 7 sts, k5, p1, k1.

Next Row (WS): K1, k1, *p5, k2; rep from * to end.

Pattern Setup Row: K1, work Adventure Cables Chart 4 (5, 6, 7, 8) times, k1.

Cont in patt as est, working first and last sts as garter and all other sts in the Adventure Cables Pattern, for 109 more rows, working Rows 2–48 once, 1–48 once, and 1–14 once, ending with a WS Row 14 of chart.

Sleeve Shaping
Next Row (RS): CO 28 sts using the Backward Loop Method, k29, cont Row 15 of the Adventure Cables Chart to last stitch, k1—142 (170, 198, 226, 254) sts.

Next Row (WS): CO 28 sts using the Backward Loop Method, k1, p28, cont Row 16 of the Adventure Cables Chart to last 29 sts, purl to last stitch, k1—170 (198, 226, 254, 282) sts.

Pattern Setup Row: K1, work Row 17 of the Adventure Cables Chart 6 (7, 8, 9, 10) times, k1.

Cont in patt as est, working first and last sts as garter and all other sts in the Adventure Cables Pattern, for 47 (55, 71, 75, 77) more rows, working Rows 18–48 once and Rows 1–16 (24, 40, 44, 46) once.

Next Row (RS): BO 61 (73, 86, 99, 112) sts, place removable marker into edge of work, BO 48 (52, 54, 56, 58) sts, place removable marker into edge of work, BO rem sts.

Odessa Tee Adventure Cables Pattern

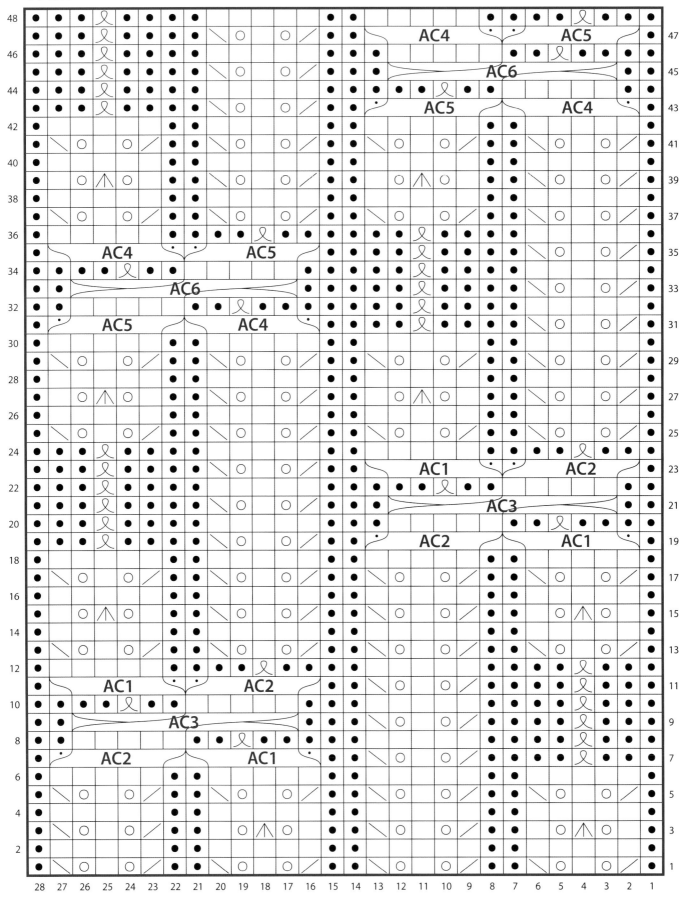

Stitches

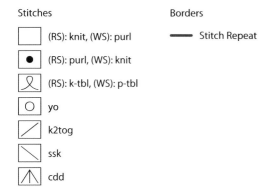

(RS): knit, (WS): purl

● (RS): purl, (WS): knit

(RS): k-tbl, (WS): p-tbl

O yo

/ k2tog

\ ssk

/\ cdd

Borders

— Stitch Repeat

CHART TIPS

Worked flat (read from right to left for RS rows, left to right for WS rows).

Uses Adventure Cables (AC) worked with lace sts.

Entire chart is repeated indicated # of times.

Chart rows are repeatable for pattern length adjustment.

Chart is repeatable for a larger garment.

Adventure Cables (AC) Stitches
Stitches are noted in pattern after being crossed.

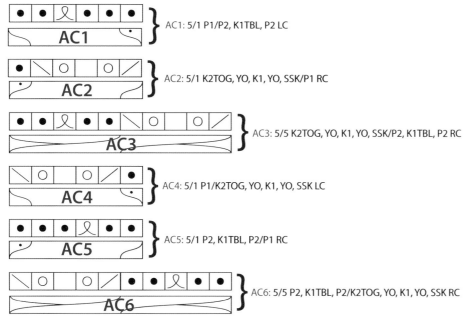

AC1: 5/1 P1/P2, K1TBL, P2 LC

AC2: 5/1 K2TOG, YO, K1, YO, SSK/P1 RC

AC3: 5/5 K2TOG, YO, K1, YO, SSK/P2, K1TBL, P2 RC

AC4: 5/1 P1/K2TOG, YO, K1, YO, SSK LC

AC5: 5/1 P2, K1TBL, P2/P1 RC

AC6: 5/5 P2, K1TBL, P2/K2TOG, YO, K1, YO, SSK RC

Front

Work same as Back through ** Pattern Setup Row**.

Cont in patt as est, working first and last sts as garter and all other sts in the Adventure Cables Pattern, for 25 (33, 45, 49, 51) more rows.

Size 42 in./106.5 cm only: Work Rows 18–42 once.

Sizes – (52½, 63, 73½, 84) in./– (133.5, 160, 186.5, 213.5) cm only: Work Rows 18–48 once, and then work Rows – (1–2, 1–14, 1–18, 1–20) once.

Neck Shaping (RS): Work 73 (87, 101, 115, 129) sts in patt, BO 24 sts, work to end in patt—73 (87, 101, 115, 129) sts on each side.

Right Front (WS): K1, work to end in patt.

BO 3 sts at beg of next 4 (4, 5, 5, 5) RS rows—61 (75, 86, 100, 114) sts.

Then BO 0 (2, 0, 1, 2) at beg of next RS row once—61 (73, 86, 99, 112) sts.

Work even for 12 more rows. BO all sts on RS.

Left Front (WS): Reattach yarn to work across WS, work to last st in patt, k1.

Next Row (RS): K1, work to end in patt.

BO 3 sts at beg of next 4 (4, 5, 5, 5) WS rows—61 (75, 86, 100, 114) sts.

Then BO 0 (2, 0, 1, 2) sts at beg of next WS row once—61 (73, 86, 99, 112) sts.

Work even for 11 more rows. BO all sts on RS.

Seaming

Wet block front and back to measurements, let dry. Using tapestry needle seam fronts to back from hem up side and under sleeve. Seam tops of sleeves from cuff to marked st at center back.

Collar

Using smaller 24 in./61 cm circular needle and starting at the right shoulder seam, pick up and knit 48 (52, 54, 56, 58) sts across back neck bind-off, 6 sts to front shaping, 12 (14, 15, 16, 17) across shaping, 24 across front bind-off, 12 (14, 15, 16, 17) across front shaping, and 6 sts to shoulder seam—108 (116, 120, 124, 128) sts. Join to work in the rnd and pm to indicate beg of rnd.

Rnd 1: Purl around.

Rnd 2: Knit around.

Rep Rnds 1–2 once more. Rep Rnd 1 once more. Loosely BO all sts knitwise.

Cuffs

Using smaller dpns and starting at the under sleeve seam, pick up and knit 84 (95, 115, 120, 123) sts, join to work in the rnd, and pm to indicate beg of rnd.

Rnd 1: Purl around.

Rnd 2: Knit around.

Rep Rnds 1–2 once more. Rep Rnd 1 once more. Loosely BO all sts knitwise.

Finishing

Work in any loose ends using tapestry needle.

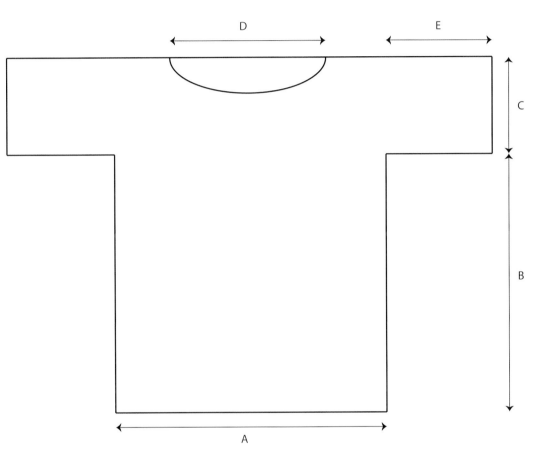

All measurements are after wet blocking, drying, and relaxing for 24 hours.

A: 22 (27.25, 32.75, 38.25, 43.5) in.
   56 (69, 83, 97, 110.5) cm
B: 18.25 in./46.5 cm
C: 7.5 (8.75, 11.25, 12, 12.25) in.
   19 (22, 28.5, 30.5, 31) cm
D: 9.25 (10, 10.5, 10.75, 11.25) in.
   23.5 (25.5, 26.5, 27.5, 28.5) cm
E: 6 in./15 cm

Palouse Falls Shawl

Flowing top down from cast-on, the Palouse Falls Shawl has double increases on the right-hand side of every right-side row to create a curl shawl in a deep golden yellow. The textured lace Adventure Cables move the single twisted knit stitch across a lacy background.

Curl shawls are one of my favorite shapes. They are easy to wear and form a striking curved shape that drapes beautifully around your neck and shoulders; they fit nicely on a variety of body shapes and sizes. For this stitch pattern, I became really interested in how to move a single twisted stitch across the work and the difference in look when moved across lace stitches or moved across purl stitches. With the single twisted stitch columns, added smocked stitches, and stacked rows of eyelets, I feel like the resulting pattern is reminiscent of waving wild grasses, gently leaning in the draft from the rumbling spray of the waterfall.

Finished Size
72¾ in./185 cm wide and 44½ in./113 cm tall

Yarn
Valley Yarns Huntington (#1 super fine weight; 75% superwash merino wool, 25% nylon; 218 yd./199 m per 1.7 oz./50 g): 5 skeins #0024 mustard

Needles
US size 5 (3.75 mm): 32 in./81 cm circular. Adjust needle size if necessary to obtain the correct gauge.

Notions
1 marker (m), cable needle (cn) optional, tapestry needle

Gauge
17 sts and 31½ rows = 4 in./10 cm in main body pattern after blocking

25 sts and 28 rows = 5 in./12.5 cm over Adventure Cables Lace Pattern

Adventure level/Advanced Intermediate: This pattern has moderate patterning on the Adventure Cable such as increases, decreases, or slipped stitches.

Pattern Notes

This shawl is worked by casting on a narrow section of stockinette stitch edged with a single garter stitch and working for the width of the vertical lace panel. Stitches are picked up from the edge of this section for the lace panel, and the shawl is worked from the top down with double yarn over increases at the beginning of every RS row to create the curl shape. The border pattern is worked evenly over all stitches.

Stitch Guide

Smocked Stitch: Following stitch column for the next st (center st in lace motif), reach right needle tip down 3 rows and insert into middle of st, wrap and pull through, k1 (center st in lace motif), reach right needle tip down 3 rows and insert into middle of st in same location as 1st st, wrap and pull through—2 sts made. *See Photo Tutorial on page 84.*

1/1/1 K1TBL/P1/K1TBL RC with cn: Slip the first 2 sts to cn and hold in back, k1tbl, slip 2 sts back to left needle, slip 1st st to cn and hold in front, p1, k1tbl from cn.

1/1/1 K1TBL/P1/K1TBL RC without cn: Reach right tip in front of work and insert into 3rd st from left tip, slip 3 sts off left tip, reinsert left tip into stitches 1 and 2 in back of work, and then place stitch 3 onto left tip, k1tbl. Reach right tip behind work and insert into 2nd stitch from left tip, slip 2 sts off left tip, reinsert left tip into dropped stitch in front of work, p1 from cn, k1tbl from left tip. *See Photo Tutorial on page 87.*

Adventure Cables Stitch Guide
With Cable Needle
AC1: 1/2 P2TOG, YO/K1TBL LC with cn: Slip 1 st to cn and hold in front, p2tog, yo, and then k1tbl from cn.

AC2: 1/2 K1TBL/YO, P2TOG RC with cn: Slip 2 sts to cn and hold in back, k1tbl, yo, p2tog from cn.

AC3: 1/2 K1TBL/P2TOG, YO RC with cn: Slip 2 sts to cn and hold in back, k1tbl, p2tog, yo from cn.

AC4: 1/2 YO, P2TOG/K1TBL LC with cn: Slip 1 st to cn and hold in front, yo, p2tog, and then k1tbl from cn.

Without Cable Needle
AC1: 1/2 P2TOG, YO/K1TBL LC without cn: Reach right needle tip behind work and insert into the 2nd and 3rd sts from left tip, slide all 3 sts off left tip, reinsert left tip into 1st st in front of work, slide 2 sts from right tip back to left tip, p2tog, yo, k1tbl.

AC2: 1/2 K1TBL/YO, P2TOG RC without cn: Reach right needle tip in front of work

and insert into the 3rd st from left tip, slide all 3 sts off left tip, reinsert left tip into 1st and 2nd sts in back of work, slide 1 st from right tip back to left tip, k1tbl, yo, p2tog.

AC3: 1/2 K1TBL/P2TOG, YO RC without cn: Reach right needle tip in front of work and insert into 3rd st from left tip, slide all 3 sts off left tip, reinsert left tip into 1st and 2nd sts in back of work, slide 1 st from right tip back to left tip, k1tbl, p2tog, yo.

AC4: 1/2 YO, P2TOG/K1TBL LC without cn: Reach right needle tip behind work and insert into the 2nd and 3rd sts from left tip, slide all 3 sts off left tip, reinsert left tip into 1st st in front of work, slide 2 sts from right tip back to left tip, yo, p2tog, k1tbl.

INSTRUCTIONS

Stockinette Border
CO 4 sts.

Row 1 (RS): K4.

Row 2 (WS): K1, p3.

Rep Rows 1–2, 24 more times.

Next Row (RS): K4, turn work ¼ turn clockwise, pick up and knit 25 sts along side, turn work ¼ turn clockwise, pick up and knit 4 sts along cast-on edge, turn work—33 sts.

Next Row (WS): P3, k1, [p1, k3, p1, k5] twice, p1, k3, p1, k1, pm, p3.

Main Body
Pattern Setup Row (RS): K3, work Increase Pattern (See Increase Chart) to m, sm, p1, work Adventure Cables Pattern to last 4 sts, p1, k3—35 sts.

Next Row (WS): P3, k1, work Adventure Cables Pattern to 1 st before marker, k1, sm, work Increase Pattern to last 3 sts, p3.

Cont in patt as est, working first and last 3 sts as stockinette, 1 st on either side of Adventure Cables Pattern as reverse stockinette, and progressing through Rows 2–28 of Increase Pattern and Adventure Cables Pattern once. Then work Rows 1–28 of the Adventure Cables Pattern 8 times more and AT THE SAME TIME work Rows 15–28 of the Increase Pattern 16 more times—313 sts.

Bottom Border
Row 1 (RS): K3, sm, *p3, work Adventure Cables Pattern; rep from * to m, sm, p1, work Adventure Cables Pattern to last 4 sts, p1, k3.

Row 2 (WS): P3, sm, k1, work Adventure Cables Pattern to 1 st before m, k1, sm, *work Adventure Cables Pattern, k3; rep from * to last 3 sts, p3.

Cont in patt as est, progressing through Adventure Cables Pattern, working first and last 3 sts in stockinette and all other sts as reverse stockinette for 32 more rows, Rows 1–28, and Rows 1–6 of Adventure Cables Pattern completed for border area.

Knit 1 row, and then BO all sts using the knitted method on the next WS row. To work knitted BO: k2, *slip both stitches back to left needle tip, k2tog tbl, knit next stitch; rep from * for remaining stitches.

Finishing
Wet block shawl to measurements using blocking wires and pins, and weave in ends using a yarn needle.

Palouse Falls Shawl Adventure Cables Pattern

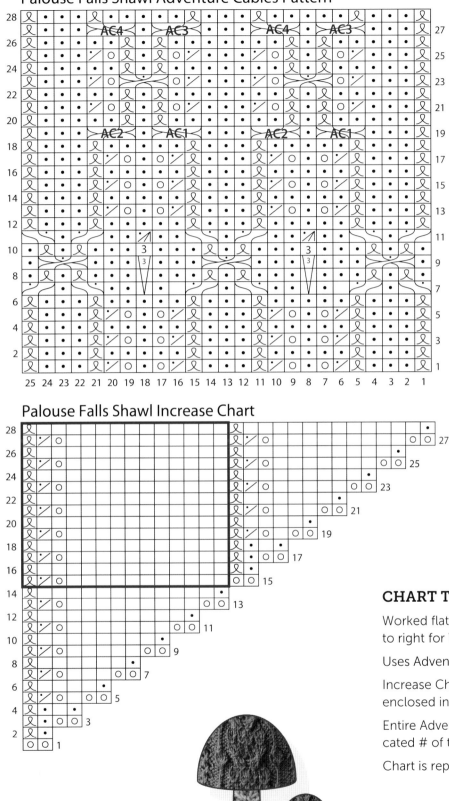

Palouse Falls Shawl Increase Chart

Stitches

- ☐ RS: k; WS: p
- • RS: p; WS: k
- ℓ RS: k-tbl; WS: p-tbl
- ○ yo
- ⟋ p2tog
- ⟋ p3tog
- 1/1 RPC
- 1/1 LPC
- 1/1/1 K1TBL/P1/K1TBL RC
- ③ WS: purl 3
- ③ Smocked Stitch: see pattern notes
- WS: knit 1
- RS: purl 1

Borders

— Stitch Repeat

Adventure Cables (AC) Stitches

Stitches are noted in pattern after being crossed.

} AC1: 1/2 P2TOG, YO/K1TBL LC

} AC2: 1/2 K1TBL/YO, P2TOG RC

} AC3: 1/2 K1TBL/P2TOG,YO RC

} AC4: 1/2 YO, P2TOG/K1TBL LC

CHART TIPS

Worked flat (read from right to left for RS rows, left to right for WS rows).

Uses Adventure Cables (AC) worked with lace sts.

Increase Chart has a stitch repeat; repeat stitches enclosed in red box indicated # of times.

Entire Adventure Cables Chart is repeated indicated # of times.

Chart is repeatable for a larger shawl.

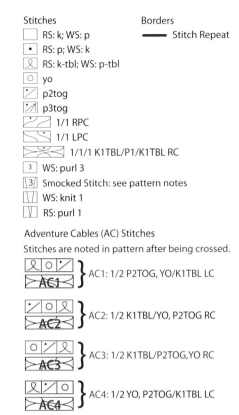

TUTORIAL: How to Work a Smocked Texture Stitch

The Palouse Falls Shawl uses a stitch called the Smocked Texture Stitch. This stitch is worked by knitting down into the center stitch a few rows below the active stitches and bringing the active yarn up. This is worked before and after the active center stitch, creating one more stitch on either side of the center stitch. The three stitches from one are worked for a single wrong-side row before being decreased on the following right side back to the single center stitch. You can see a completed smocked stitch to the right; it looks like a tiny flower of gathered stitches.

On the chart, this stitch is a specialty stitch that increases from 1 to 3 stitches and is shown on one single grid square. The smocked stitch has active patterning on 3 rows of the chart: reaching down to create stitches, working them as purl stitches on the wrong side, and decreasing them with a purl 3 together. But the stitch is actually shown over 5 rows of the chart since the charted pattern includes the 2 rows that the right needle tip needs to reach down to pick up the stitches.

Tip: As long as you are consistently picking up the stitches from the same row for every smocked stitch, it's not terribly important that you pick up from exactly 2 rows below. Just make a visual decision to always insert the right needle into the same area.

The smocked stitch is worked on Row 9 of the Palouse Falls Adventure Cables Chart, although the bottom of the elongated V reaches down to Row 7, indicating how far the right needle needs to reach down to create the smocked stitch.

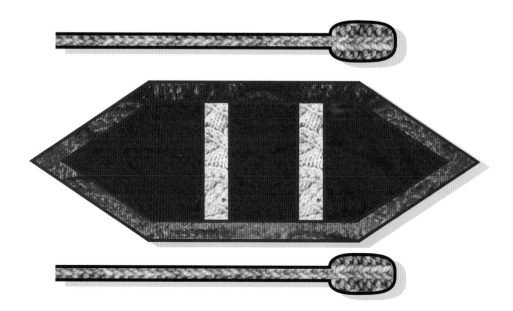

Adventure Cables Pattern

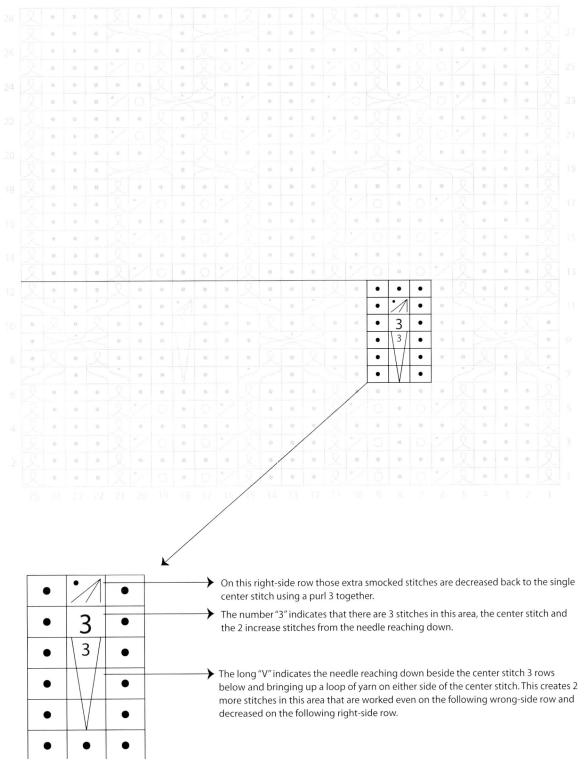

On this right-side row those extra smocked stitches are decreased back to the single center stitch using a purl 3 together.

The number "3" indicates that there are 3 stitches in this area, the center stitch and the 2 increase stitches from the needle reaching down.

The long "V" indicates the needle reaching down beside the center stitch 3 rows below and bringing up a loop of yarn on either side of the center stitch. This creates 2 more stitches in this area that are worked even on the following wrong-side row and decreased on the following right-side row.

1. On Row 9, work through stitch 7 (stitch 7 is completed as a purl stitch and is located on the right-hand needle; stitch 8 is on the left-hand needle waiting to be worked).

2. Reach right needle tip down 3 rows and insert into the center stitch. The needle will pass 3 purl bumps as you reach down.

3. Wrap the yarn around the right needle tip and bring up a stitch.

4. Now purl the center stitch.

5. Again, reach right needle tip down 3 rows and insert into the center stitch. This will be exactly the same spot that the first smocked stitch was worked into.

6. Wrap the right needle and pull through. There are now 3 stitches instead of one center stitch.

7. On the following wrong-side row, work these stitches as p3; on the following right side, p3tog.

TUTORIAL: How to Work a 1/1/1 K1TBL/P1/K1TBL RC

This 3-stitch twisted cable is worked on Rows 9 and 23 of the Palouse Falls Adventure Cables Chart. This stitch is best worked without a cable needle, as the movement of the single stitches in a lace weight yarn is difficult to perform with a cable needle. This cable is worked by first rearranging all 3 stitches and then working across them as k1tbl, p1, k1tbl.

1. On Row 9, work through stitch 1, ready to work the cable over stitches 2, 3, and 4.

2. Reach right tip in front of work and insert into 3rd stitch from left tip.

3. Slip 3 sts off left tip, reinsert left tip into stitches 1 and 2 in back of work.

4. Reach right tip behind work and insert into 2nd stitch from left tip.

5. Slip 2 sts off left tip, reinsert left tip into dropped stitch in front of work.

6. Slip 2 sts from right needle tip to left needle tip, work across stitches as k1tbl, p1, k1tbl.

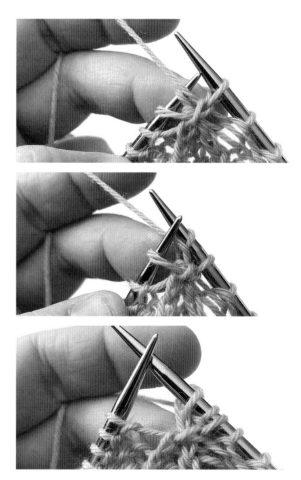

Bainbridge Wrap

A wide panel of lace over lace crossings is complemented by a main body of welted stitches in the Bainbridge Wrap. Every Adventure Cable uses 4 lace stitches crossed over either purl or knit stitches. Sections of extra-large eyelets are worked parallel to the Adventure Cables on the right-hand side of the wrap, giving the finished piece a balanced composition.

I love a rectangular wrap since it can be worn on the shoulders or as a large scarf, and designing one is more like creating a painting or drawing than a knitting design. For this stitch pattern, I wanted to emulate water, twisting and flowing around itself in a circular convection current. The upper narrow border reminds me of the horizon line, and the welted patterning is like rows and rows of rippled sandbars reaching out into the swirling water (sample knit by Gretchen Cunningham).

Finished Size
19 ¾ in./50 cm tall and 56½ in./143.5 cm wide

Yarn
Sweet Georgia Yarns Cashluxe Fine (#1 super fine weight; 70% merino wool, 20% cashmere, 10% nylon; 400 yd./366 m per 4 oz./112 g): 3 skeins Westwind

Needles
US size 6 (4.0 mm): 32 in./81 cm circular. Adjust needle size if necessary to obtain the correct gauge.

Notions
3 markers (m), cable needle (cn) optional, tapestry needle

Gauge
24½ sts and 30 rows = 4 in./10 cm in Welted Body Pattern, after blocking

28 sts and 28¾ rows = 4 in./10 cm over Adventure Cables Lace Pattern

Adventure level/Advanced Intermediate: This pattern has moderate patterning on the Adventure Cables such as increases, decreases, or slipped stitches.

Pattern Notes

This shawl is worked flat back and forth. Double yarn overs are worked as a knit and a purl on the wrong side, creating 2 stitches out of the double-wrapped stitch.

Alteration Information

Note: Any alterations made may affect yardage amounts used.

- ✳ To increase width on this shawl, it is best to add stitches in the welted area; any multiple of stitches can be added here.
- ✳ To increase length, add or subtract row repeats as desired.

Stitch Guide

Welted Pattern
Rows 1, 3, 5, 7, 10, 12, 14, and 16: Knit.

Rows 2, 4, 6, 8, 9, 11, 13, and 15: Purl.

Rep these 16 rows for patt.

Double Eyelet Pattern
Row 1 (RS): P2, k2tog, yo, yo, ssk, p2.

Row 2 (WS): K2, p2, k1, p1, k2.

Rows 3, 5, and 7: P2, k4, p2.

Rows 4, 6, and 8: K2, p4, k2.

Rep these 8 rows for patt.

4/1 LPC: Slip the first 4 sts to cn and hold in front, p1, k4 from cn.

4/1 RPC: Slip the 1st st to cn and hold in back, k4, p1 from cn.

Adventure Cables Stitch Guide
With Cable Needle
AC1: 4/1 K2, YO, SSK/P1 RC with cn: Slip 1 st to cn and hold in back, k2, yo, ssk, and then p1 from cn.

AC2: 4/1 P1/K2, YO, SSK LC with cn: Slip 4 sts to cn and hold in front, p1, and then k2, yo, ssk from cn.

AC3: 4/4 K2, YO, SSK/K4 RC with cn: Slip 4 sts to cn and hold in back, k2, yo, ssk, and then k4 from cn.

AC4: 4/4 K4/K2, YO, SSK LC with cn: Slip 4 sts to cn and hold in front, k4, and then k2, yo, ssk from cn.

AC5: 4/2 K2, YO, SSK/P2 **RC** with cn: Slip 2 sts to cn and hold in back, k2, yo, ssk, and then p2 from cn.

AC6: 4/2 P2/K2, YO, SSK **LC** with cn: Slip 4 sts to cn and hold in front, p2, and then k2, yo, ssk from cn.

Without Cable Needle

AC1: 4/1 K2, YO, SSK/P1 **RC** without cn: Reach right needle tip in front of work and insert into the 2nd, 3rd, 4th, and 5th sts from left tip, slide all 5 sts off left tip, reinsert left tip into 1st st in back of work, slide 4 sts from right tip back to left tip, k2, yo, ssk, p1.

AC2: 4/1 P1/K2, YO, SSK **LC** without cn: Reach right needle tip behind work and insert into the 5th st from left tip, slide all 5 sts off left tip, reinsert left tip into first 4 sts in front of work, slide 1 st from right tip back to left tip, p1, k2, yo, ssk.

AC3: 4/4 K2, YO, SSK/K4 **RC** without cn: Reach right needle tip in front of work and insert into the 5th, 6th, 7th, and 8th sts from left tip, slide all 8 sts off left tip, reinsert left tip into first 4 sts in back of work, slide 4 sts from right tip back to left tip, k2, yo, ssk, k4.

AC4: 4/4 K4/K2, YO, SSK **LC** without cn: Reach right needle tip in back of work and insert into the 5th, 6th, 7th, and 8th sts from left tip, slide all 8 sts off left tip, reinsert left tip into first 4 sts in front of work, slide 4 sts from right tip back to left tip, k4, k2, yo, ssk.

AC5: 4/2 K2, YO, SSK/P2 **RC** without cn: Reach right needle tip in front of work and insert into the 3rd, 4th, 5th, and 6th sts from left tip, slide all 6 sts off left tip, reinsert left tip into first 2 sts in back of work, slide 4 sts from right tip back to left tip, k2, yo, ssk, p2.

AC6: 4/2 P2/K2, YO, SSK **LC** without cn: Reach right needle tip in back of work and insert into the 5th and 6th sts from left tip, slide all 6 sts off left tip, reinsert left tip into first 4 sts in front of work, slide 2 sts from right tip back to left tip, p2, k2, yo, ssk.

INSTRUCTIONS

CO 130 sts using the Old Norwegian method (*see Tutorial on page 39*) or an equally stretchy method of your choice.

Knit 5 rows.

Setup Row (WS): K5, pm, k70, pm, k32, pm, k8, pm, k15.

Pattern Setup Row (RS): Work Welted Pattern to m, sm, work Double Eyelet Pattern to m, sm, work Welted Pattern to m, sm, work Adventure Cables Pattern to m, sm, work Welted Pattern to end.

Cont in patt as est for 405 more rows, progressing through Rows 2–16 of Welted Pattern, 2–8 of Double Eyelet Pattern, and 2–64 of Adventure Cables Pattern once. Then rep Rows 1–16 of Welted Pattern 24 more times. Rep Rows 1–8 of Double Eyelet Pattern 49 more times, and Rows 1–64 of Adventure Cables Pattern 5 more times. Then work Rows 1–6 of Welted Pattern and Double Eyelet Pattern once more, and Rows 1–22 of Adventure Cables Pattern once more.

Border
Knit 5 rows.

BO all sts knitwise on WS row.

Finishing
Wet block shawl to measurements using blocking wires and pins. Weave in ends using a yarn needle.

Bainbridge Wrap Adventure Cables Chart

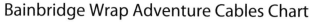

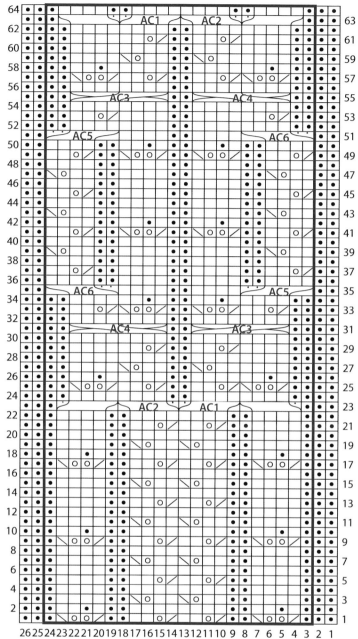

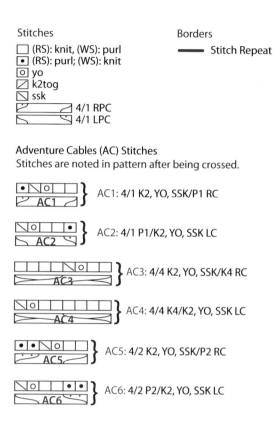

Stitches

☐ (RS): knit, (WS): purl
● (RS): purl; (WS): knit
○ yo
╱ k2tog
╲ ssk
4/1 RPC
4/1 LPC

Borders

── Stitch Repeat

Adventure Cables (AC) Stitches
Stitches are noted in pattern after being crossed.

} AC1: 4/1 K2, YO, SSK/P1 RC

} AC2: 4/1 P1/K2, YO, SSK LC

} AC3: 4/4 K2, YO, SSK/K4 RC

} AC4: 4/4 K4/K2, YO, SSK LC

} AC5: 4/2 K2, YO, SSK/P2 RC

} AC6: 4/2 P2/K2, YO, SSK LC

CHART TIPS

Worked flat (read from right to left for RS rows, left to right for WS rows).

Uses cables worked with knit and purl sts.

Uses Adventure Cables (AC) worked with lace sts.

Has a stitch repeat; repeat stitches enclosed in red box indicated # of times.

Chart rows are repeatable for pattern length adjustment.

CHAPTER
CABLE
CROSSINGS

CROSSINGS WITH

CABLED STITCHES

Cables are traditionally defined as crossing sets of stitches to create texture and graphic motifs. Adventure Cables take this idea one step further and include moving sets of stitches to create cables and moving sets of cabled stitches to create deeply textured and layered cables.

This chapter starts with the Woods Creek Shawl, which has traditional cables that are then moved over top of a lace pattern, while the Point Defiance Pullover has traditional cables that are moved over each other. Both these patterns work the Adventure Cables with either simple lace or texture stitches, further building on skills acquired in the first two chapters. The final three patterns in this chapter—Roxboro Mittens, Goose Prairie Vest, and Seven Bays Cardigan—are all worked with cabled stitches during the Adventure Cables. The patterns in this chapter all boast deep texture and layers of cables; matching gauge is especially important for this chapter, as the work pulls in a great deal more than expected.

WHAT TO EXPECT

The "Crossings with Cable Stitches" chapter includes moving large cable motifs across each other on non-cabling rows and working them with knits and purls like the texture chapter. It also includes moving cabled stitches across each other or around each other on cable pattern rows, thus working the Adventure Cable and the cable pattern stitches at the same time.

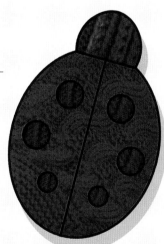

SKILL LEVELS INCLUDED

"Crossings with Cable Stitches" includes two Explore level patterns where the Adventure Cable takes place over knit and purl stitches, and three Be Brave level patterns where the Adventure Cable takes place during a cable pattern row.

Woods Creek Shawl

The Woods Creek Shawl crosses cabled columns and lace stitches for an optical illusion of cable circles on top of lace circles. This shawl is worked top down with three wedges of Adventure Cable patterning and finished with a wide border of garter stitch.

This stitch pattern was a bit of a shawl shape surprise. Since so many of the stitches are crossed over each other, it pulled the yarn into a narrower shape than the traditional triangle shawl. I decided to take advantage of this shape by repeating the pattern three times across the shawl for a crescent shawl shape that for all intents and purposes should really be a ¾ square shawl! The twisting flipping lace and cables pattern worked in the red yarn took me immediately to beautiful autumn leaves floating down an icy creek just about ready for snowfall.

Explore level/Intermediate: This pattern has very simple patterning on the Adventure Cable such as knits and purls.

Finished Size
51 in./129.5 cm wide and 25½ in./65 cm tall

Yarn
Plymouth Yarn Company R.S.S. Reserve Sport Solid (#2 fine weight; 45% extra fine merino wool, 35% mulberry silk, 20% bamboo; 348 yd./318 m per 3.5 oz./100 g): 3 skeins #0005 Red Velvet

Needles
US size 6 (4.0 mm): 32 in./81 cm circular. Adjust needle size if necessary to obtain the correct gauge.

Notions
2 markers (m), cable needle (cn) optional, tapestry needle

Gauge
19 sts and 24 rows = 4 in./10 cm over Adventure Cables Lace Pattern, after blocking

19½ sts and 34 rows = 4 in./10 cm in garter stitch, after blocking

Pattern Notes

This shawl is worked by casting on a narrow border of garter stitch and working a garter stitch "tab" to pick up from. Because the Adventure Cables patterning in this pattern uses cabled stitches that are also crossed, it pulls in more than a typical pattern. For this reason, the wedge shapes that increase 2 stitches every right-side row are narrower than the typical 90-degree shape. Three wedges are worked for a shawl that is slightly more than 180 degrees, with 6 stitches increased on each right-side row (one on either side of each of three pattern wedges). The garter stitch patterning increases 25 stitches every 10 rows of work.

Stitch Guide

1/2 LC: Slip 1 st to cn and hold in front, k2, k1 from cn.

1/2 RC: Slip 2 sts to cn and hold in back, k1, k2 from cn.

K3/P1, K2 RC: Slip 3 sts to cn and hold in back, k3, and then p1, k2 from cn.

K2, P1/K3 LC: Slip 3 sts to cn and hold in front, k2, p1, and then k3 from cn.

INSTRUCTIONS

Garter Tab

CO 3 sts.

Knit 16 rows.

Next Row (RS): K3, turn work ¼ turn clockwise, pick up and knit 8 sts along side, turn work ¼ turn clockwise, pick up and knit 3 sts along cast-on edge—14 sts. Turn work.

Next Row (WS): K3, [p3, pm] twice, p2, k3.

Cables and Lace Pattern 1

Pattern Setup Row (RS): K3, [work Cables and Lace Pattern 1 to m, sm, k1] twice, work Cables and Lace Pattern 1 to last 3 sts, k3—6 sts inc'd.

Next Row (WS): K3, [work Cables and Lace Pattern 1 to 1 st before m, p1, sm] twice, work Cables and Lace Pattern 1 to last 3 sts, k3.

Cont in patt as est progressing through Rows 3–24 of Cables and Lace Pattern 1—86 sts.

Cables and Lace Pattern 2

Pattern Setup Row (RS): K3, [work Cables and Lace Pattern 2 to m, sm, k1] twice, work Cables and Lace Pattern 2 to last 3 sts, k3—6 sts inc'd.

Next Row (WS): K3, [work Cables and Lace Pattern 2 to 1 st before m, p1, sm] twice, work Cables and Lace Pattern 2 to last 3 sts, k3.

Cont in patt as est progressing through Rows 3–24 of Cables and Lace Pattern 2 once, and then repeating Rows 1–24 three more times—374 sts.

Border

Knit 8 rows even.

Inc Row (RS): K7, [k1fb, k14] 24 times, k1fb, k6—399 sts.

Knit 9 rows even.

Inc Row (RS): K7, [k1fb, k15] 24 times, k1fb, k7—424 sts.

Knit 9 rows even.

Inc Row (RS): K7, [k1fb, k16] 24 times, k1fb, k8—449 sts.

Knit 4 rows even.

BO all sts on WS.

Finishing

Wet block shawl to measurements using blocking wires and pins; weave in ends using a yarn needle.

CHART TIPS

Worked flat (read from right to left for RS rows, left to right for WS rows).

Uses Adventure Cables (AC) worked with knit and purl sts.

Has a stitch repeat; repeat stitches enclosed in red box indicated # of times.

Chart rows are repeatable for pattern length adjustment.

Chart is repeatable for a larger shawl.

Woods Creek Shawl Cables and Lace Pattern 1

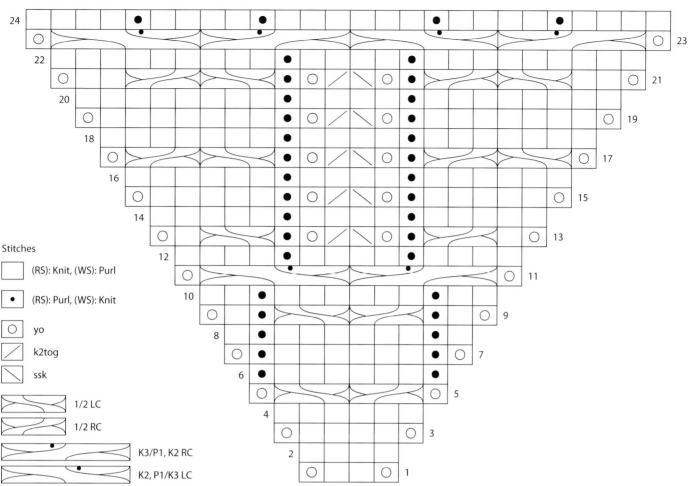

Stitches

☐	(RS): Knit, (WS): Purl
•	(RS): Purl, (WS): Knit
○	yo
╱	k2tog
╲	ssk
	1/2 LC
	1/2 RC
	K3/P1, K2 RC
	K2, P1/K3 LC

Woods Creek Shawl Cables and Lace Pattern 2

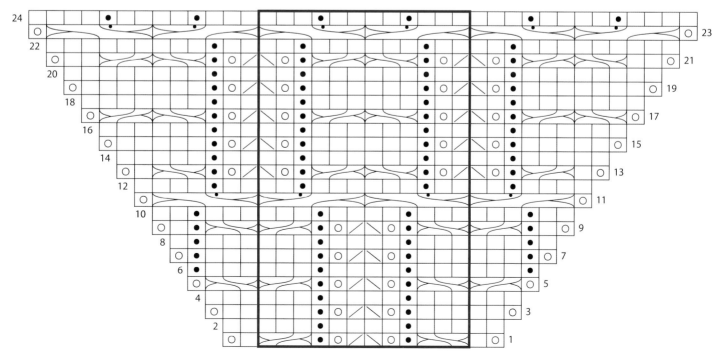

Point Defiance Pullover

A wide bottom border of Adventure Cables based on ribbing and punctuated with bobbles makes for a deeply textured beginning to this quintessential pullover. The deep V-neck is a classic look while the relaxed drop-shoulder shaping keeps this boxy knit casual and comfy.

This stitch pattern was the first Adventure Cable experiment that I conducted, and I really fell in love with the layers of texture that were achieved with the ribbing, bobbles, and cables. But creating an entire garment out of the stitch pattern seemed like it would be too bulky to wear, so again a combination of intricate stitch pattern and simple texture was needed. The deep gold and flickering cables are perfect for a singalong around the evening campfire.

Explore level/Intermediate: This pattern has very simple patterning on the Adventure Cable such as knits and purls.

Finished Sizes
34¾ (37¼, 42, 44½, 49½) (54½, 57, 62, 66¾, 69¼) in./88.5 (94.5, 106.5, 113, 125.5) (138.5, 145, 157.5, 169.5, 176) cm bust circumference

Shown in size 44½, modeled with 5 in./12.5 cm of positive ease.

Yarn
Berroco Ultra Wool DK (#4 medium weight; 100% superwash wool; 292 yd./267 m per 3.5 oz./100 g): 4 (5, 5, 6, 6) (7, 7, 8, 8, 9) balls #8329 Butternut

Needles
US size 6 (4.0 mm): 32 in./81 cm circular or straight needles, 16 in./41 cm circular needles, 1 set of 4 double-pointed needles (dpns)

US size 5 (3.75 mm): 24 in./61 cm circular needles

Adjust needle size if necessary to obtain the correct gauge.

Notions
2 removable markers (m), 1 stitch marker, cable needle (cn) optional, tapestry needle

Gauge
21 sts and 26 rows = 4 in./10 cm in Upper Body Pattern

20 sts and 27 rows = 4 in./10 cm in stockinette stitch

20 sts = 2½ in./6.5 cm over Adventure Cables Pattern, unstretched

Pattern Notes

This pullover is worked from the bottom up in the round to the armhole depth, and then the front and back are worked separately back and forth to the shoulders. The Lower Body cast-on has 65 percent more stitches than the Upper Body to accommodate the ribbed Adventure Cables. Gauge over the Upper Body Pattern relates to bust circumference while gauge over the Adventure Cables Chart relates to Lower Body circumference. A decrease round is worked between the Lower Body and Upper Body Patterns to reduce the stitch count and create the rib patt for the Upper Body.

Alteration Information

Note: *Any alterations made may affect yardage amounts used.*

* ✳ The body length of this garment can easily be adjusted by adding or removing length before the armhole division.
* ✳ Sleeve length can be adjusted by removing or adding rounds worked even before decreases. If a wider cuff is desired, remove decreases in sets of 2 so the cuff rib pattern will still have a multiple of 4 sts in the final count.
* ✳ Upper-arm circumference and armhole depth can be altered by using the sleeve alteration instructions on page 19.
* ✳ Altering the armhole depth for this garment will change the neck depth and the number of picked-up stitches for the collar. To calculate your new collar pickup, multiply your new armhole depth by 5 sts per inch—this is how many stitches to pick up between the bottom of the "V" and the shoulder seam for each side. Multiply this number by 2 and add the back pickup stitch count for your size; this number needs to be a multiple of 4, and you may have to add or subtract a stitch or two from each side to adjust it.

Stitch Guide

MB (make bobble): [K1, yo, k1, yo, k1] into 1 st, turn work. P5, turn work. Sl3 as if to k3tog, k2tog, pass 3 over.

Upper Body Pattern (multiple of 13)
Rnd 1: *K4, p1, k3, p1, k4; rep from * to end of rnd.

1/1 RC with cn: Slip 1 st to cn and hold in back, k1, k1 from cn.

1/1 LC with cn: Slip 1 st to cn and hold in front, k1, k1 from cn.

1/1 RPC with cn: Slip 1 st to cn and hold in back, k1, p1 from cn.

1/1 LPC with cn: Slip 1 st to cn and hold in front, p1, k1 from cn.

1/1 RC without cn: Reach right tip in front of work and insert into 2nd st from left tip, slide 2 sts off left tip, reinsert left tip into 1st st behind work, slide 1 st from right tip to left tip, k2.

1/1 LC without cn: Reach right needle tip behind work and insert into 2nd st from left tip, slide 2 sts off left tip, reinsert left tip into 1st st in front of work, slide 1 st from right tip back to left tip, k2.

1/1 RPC without cn: Reach right tip in front of work and insert into 2nd st from left tip, slide 2 sts off left tip, reinsert left tip into 1st st behind work, slide 1 st from right tip to left tip, k1, p1.

1/1 LPC without cn: Reach right needle tip behind work and insert into 2nd st from left tip, slide 2 sts off left tip, reinsert left tip into 1st st in front of work, slide 1 st from right tip back to left tip, p1, k1.

Adventure Cables Stitch Guide
With Cable Needle
AC1: 5/5 K1, P3, K1/P1, K2, P2 RC with cn: Slip 5 sts to cn and hold in back, k1, p3, k1, and then p1, k2, p2 from cn.

AC2: 5/5 P2, K2, P1/K1, P3, K1 LC with cn: Slip 5 sts to cn and hold in front, p2, k2, p1, and then k1, p3, k1 from cn.

AC3: 5/5 P1, K2, P2/K1, P3, K1 RC with cn: Slip 5 sts to cn and hold in back, p1, k2, p2, and then k1, p3, k1 from cn.

AC4: 5/5 K1, P3, K1/ P2, K2, P1 LC with cn: Slip 5 sts to cn and hold in front, k1, p3, k1, and then p2, k2, p1 from cn.

Without Cable Needle
AC1: 5/5 K1, P3, K1/P1, K2, P2 RC without cn: Reach right needle tip in front of work and insert into the 6th, 7th, 8th, 9th, and 10th sts from left tip, slide all 10 sts off left tip, reinsert left tip into 1st, 2nd, 3rd, 4th, and 5th sts behind work, slide 5 sts from right tip back to left tip, k1, p3, k1, p1, k2, p2.

AC2: 5/5 P2, K2, P1/K1, P3, K1 LC without cn: Reach right needle tip behind work and insert into the 6th, 7th, 8th, 9th, and 10th sts from left tip, slide all 10 sts off left tip, reinsert left tip into first 5 sts in front of work, slide 5 sts from right tip back to left tip, p2, k2, p1, k1, p3, k1.

AC3: 5/5 P1, K2, P2/ K1, P3, K1 RC without cn: Reach right needle tip in front of work and insert into the 6th, 7th, 8th, 9th, and 10th sts from left tip, slide all 10 sts off left tip, reinsert left tip into 1st, 2nd, 3rd, 4th, and 5th sts behind work, slide 5 sts from right tip back to left tip, p1, k2, p2, k1, p3, k1.

AC4: 5/5 K1, P3, K1/ P2, K2, P1 LC without cn: Reach right needle tip behind work and insert into the 6th, 7th, 8th, 9th, and 10th sts from left tip, slide all 10 sts off left tip, reinsert left tip into first 5 sts in front of work, slide 5 sts from right tip back to left tip, k1, p3, k1, p2, k2, p1.

INSTRUCTIONS

Lower Body

Using larger 32 in./81 cm needles, CO 280 (300, 340, 360, 400) (440, 460, 500, 540, 560) sts, join to work in the round, and place marker (pm) to indicate beg of rnd.

Rnd 1: P1 *k2, p2; rep from * to last 3 sts, k2, p1.

Rep last rnd 5 more times.

Pattern Setup Rnd: Work Adventure Cables Chart 14 (15, 17, 18, 20) (22, 23, 25, 27, 28) times around.

Cont in patt progressing through Rows 2–44 of Adventure Cables Chart.

Decrease Rnd: *K2tog, k1, k2tog, ssk, p1, k2, ssk, p1, [k2tog] twice, k1, ssk; rep from * 13 (14 16, 17, 19) (21, 22, 24, 26, 27) more times—182 (195, 221, 234, 260) (286, 299, 325, 351, 364) sts.

Next Rnd: *K4, p1, k3, p1, k4; rep from * to end of rnd.

Cont in patt as est until piece measures 15 (15, 15, 15, 16) (16, 16, 16, 16, 16) in./38 (38, 38, 38, 40.5) (40.5, 40.5, 40.5, 40.5, 40.5) cm from cast-on edge.

Divide for Armholes

Row 1 (RS): Work 91 (88, 107, 117, 123) (143, 140, 159, 166, 175) sts in patt as est, turn work.

Row 2 (WS): Work back sts in patt (as they appear, knit the knit sts and purl the purl sts) removing beg of rnd marker, and then work 0 (10, 3, 0, 6) (0, 10, 3, 10, 6) sts more in patt, turn work.

Back

Cont working flat in patt over these back sts until back measures 6¾ (7, 7½, 8¼, 9¼) (10, 10¾, 11, 11¼, 11½) in./17 (18, 19, 21, 23.5) (25.5, 27.5, 28, 28.5, 29) cm from armhole division.

Shoulder Shaping: BO 8 (8, 10, 11, 13) (14, 15, 17, 18, 19) sts at beg of next 4 rows—59 (66, 70, 73, 77) (87, 90, 94, 104, 105) sts rem.

BO 9 (10, 12, 12, 13) (16, 16, 17, 20, 20) sts at beg of foll 2 rows—41 (46, 46, 49, 51) (55, 58, 60, 64, 65) sts rem.

BO all sts.

Point Defiance Adventure Cables Chart

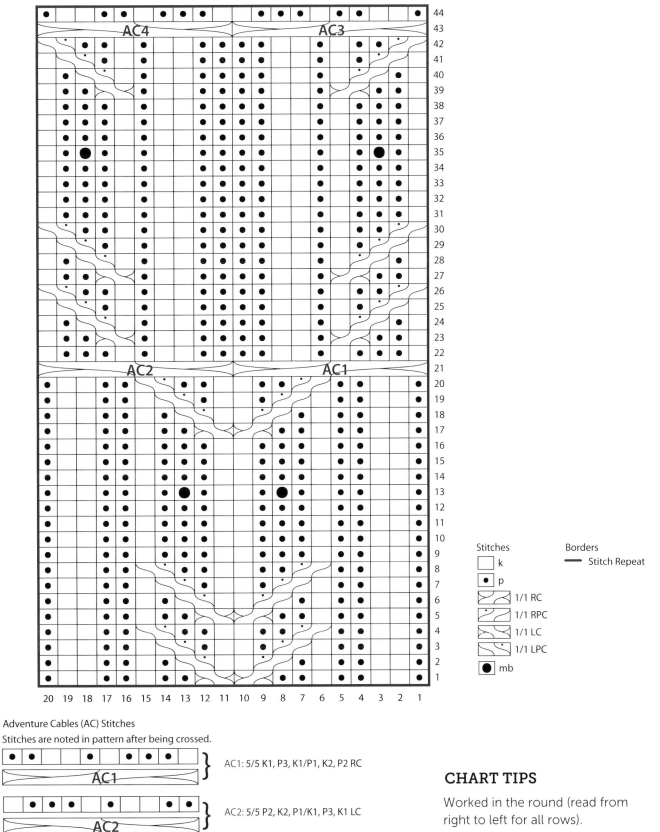

Adventure Cables (AC) Stitches

Stitches are noted in pattern after being crossed.

AC1: 5/5 K1, P3, K1/P1, K2, P2 RC

AC2: 5/5 P2, K2, P1/K1, P3, K1 LC

AC3: 5/5 P1, K2, P2/K1, P3, K1 RC

AC4: 5/5 K1, P3, K1/P2, K2, P1 LC

Stitches

☐ k

● p

1/1 RC

1/1 RPC

1/1 LC

1/1 LPC

● mb

Borders

— Stitch Repeat

CHART TIPS

Worked in the round (read from right to left for all rows).

Uses Adventure Cables (AC) worked with knit and purl sts.

Entire chart is repeated indicated # of times.

Front
Reattach yarn to work across RS of rem 91 (97, 111, 117, 131) (143, 149, 163, 175, 183) sts.

Left Front
Row 1 (RS): Work across 42 (45, 51, 55, 61) (68, 71, 77, 84, 87) sts in patt as est, ssk, k2, turn work—1 st decreased.

Row 2 (WS): K1, work sts as they appear to last st, k1.

Dec Row (RS): Work in patt as est to last 4 sts, ssk, k2—1 st decreased at neck edge.

Rep Dec Row every RS row 19 (20, 21, 23, 24) (26, 27, 28, 30, 31) more times—25 (27, 32, 34, 39) (44, 46, 51, 56, 58) sts.

Work even if necessary until piece measures 6¾ (7, 7½, 8¼, 9¼) (10, 10¾, 11, 11¼, 11½) in./17 (17.75, 19, 21, 23.5) (25, 27.25, 28, 28.5, 29.25) cm from armhole division, ending with a WS row.

Shoulder Shaping: BO 8 (8, 10, 11, 13) (14, 15, 17, 18, 19) sts at the beg of next 3 RS rows. BO any rem sts.

Right Front
Reattach yarn to work across RS of rem Right Front sts.

Dec Row (RS): K2, k2tog, work to end in patt—1 st decreased at neck edge.

Row 2 (WS): K1, work sts as they appear to last st, k1.

Rep Dec Row every RS row 18 (20, 21, 22, 24) (25, 27, 28, 30, 31) more times—25 (27, 32, 34, 39) (44, 46, 51, 56, 58) sts.

Work even if necessary until piece measures 6¾ (7, 7½, 8¼, 9¼) (10, 10¾, 11, 11¼, 11½) in./17 (17.75, 19, 21, 23.5) (25, 27.25, 28, 28.5, 29.25) cm from armhole division, ending with a RS row.

Shoulder Shaping: BO 8 (8, 10, 11, 13) (14, 15, 17, 18, 19) sts at the beg of next 3 WS rows. BO any rem sts.

Seaming
Using tapestry needle, seam Fronts to Back at shoulder.

Sleeves
Using 16 in./41 cm circular needle, pick up and knit 70 (74, 78, 86, 96) (104, 112, 116, 118, 120) sts evenly around armhole opening, join to work in the round, and pm (place marker) for beg of rnd.

Knit 8 (16, 9, 8, 6) (6, 2, 14, 11, 4) rnds even.

Dec Rnd: K1, k2tog, knit to last 3 sts, ssk, k1—2 sts decreased.

Rep Dec Rnd every 10 (8, 7, 6, 5) (4, 4, 3, 3, 3) rnds 10 (12, 14, 16, 21) (25, 27, 29, 28, 29) more times—48 (48, 48, 52, 52) (52, 56, 56, 60, 60) sts.

Take a minute to try on the sweater at this point to see how the sleeve fits before continuing to add extra length. You may want to skip straight to the cuff.

Work even to 18 (18, 18, 18, 17¾) (17½, 17, 16, 15, 14¼) in./45.75 (45.75, 45.75, 45.75, 45) (44.5, 43, 40.5, 38, 36) cm or 2 in./5 cm less than desired length.

Next Rnd: *K2, p2; rep from * around.

Rep last rnd for an additional 2 in./5 cm, BO all sts in patt.

Collar

Beg at bottom of right front opening and using smaller 24 in./61 cm circular needle, pick up and knit 35 (36, 39, 43, 48) (52, 56, 57, 59, 59) sts to shoulder seam, 42 (44, 46, 50, 52) (56, 56, 62, 66, 66) sts across back neck, and 35 (36, 39, 43, 48) (52, 56, 57, 59, 59) sts to bottom left front—112 (116, 124, 136, 148) (160, 168, 176, 184, 184) sts. Join to work in the rnd and pm for beg of rnd.

Rnd 1: K1, *p2, k2; rep from * to last 3 sts, p2, k1.

Rnd 2: Ssk, p1, *k2, p2; rep from * to last 5 sts, k2, p1, k2tog—2 sts decreased.

Rnd 3: K1, p1, *k2, p2; rep from * to last 4 sts, k2, p1, k1.

Rnd 4: Ssk, *k2, p2; rep from * to last 4 sts, k2, k2tog—2 sts decreased.

Rnd 5: K1, *k2, p2; rep from * to last 3 sts, k3.

Rnd 6: Ssk, k1, *p2, k2; rep from * to last 5 sts, p2, k1, k2tog—2 sts decreased.

Rnd 7: K2, *p2, k2; rep from * to end.

Rnd 8: Ssk, *p2, k2; rep from * to last 4 sts, p2, k2tog—2 sts decreased: 104 (108, 116, 128, 140) (152, 160, 168, 172, 176) sts.

BO all sts in patt.

Finishing

Work in any loose ends using tapestry needle.

A: 34.75 (37.25, 42, 44.5, 49.5)(54.5, 57, 62, 66.75, 69.25) in.
   88.5 (94.5, 106.5, 113, 125.5)(138.5, 145, 157.5, 169.5, 176) cm
B: 15 (15, 15, 15, 16)(16, 16, 16, 16, 16) in.
   38 (38, 38, 38, 40.5)(40.5, 40.5, 40.5, 40.5, 40.5) cm
C: 6.75 (7, 7.5, 8.25, 9.25)(10, 10.75, 11, 11.25, 11.5) in.
   17 (18, 19, 21, 23.5)(25.5, 27.5, 28, 28.5, 29) cm
D: 1 in./2.5 cm
E: 7.75 (8.5, 9, 9.25, 10)(10.5, 10.75, 11.5, 12.5, 12.5) in.
   19.5 (21.5, 23, 23.5, 25.5)(26.5, 27.5, 29, 32, 32) cm
F: 4.75 (5, 6, 6.5, 7.5)(8.5, 8.75, 9.75, 10.75, 11) in.
   12 (12.5, 15, 16.5, 19)(21.5, 22, 25, 27.5, 28) cm
G: 20 (20, 20, 20, 19.75)(19.5, 19, 18.5, 17, 16.25) in.
   51 (51, 51, 51, 50)(49.5, 48.5, 47, 43, 41.5) cm
H: 14 (14.75, 15.5, 17.25, 19.25)(20.75, 22.5, 23.25, 23.5, 24) in.
   35.5 (37.5, 39.5, 44, 49)(52.5, 57, 59, 59.5, 61) cm
I: 7.75 (8, 8.5, 9.25, 10.25)(11, 11.75, 12, 12.25, 12.5) in.
   19.5 (20.5, 21.5, 23.5, 26)(28, 30, 30.5, 31, 32) cm

Roxboro Mittens

Worked with a deeply textured combination of cabled Adventure Cables, the crossed columns of twisted stitches create a very sculptural mitten. Each lozenge-shaped cable pattern opens to reveal an additional traditional cable in the center, and the columns of twisted stitches on the side continue through the decreases to frame the whole mitten.

For these mittens, I wanted to work with two kinds of cables to show the differences between regular cables worked with stockinette and Adventure Cables with moving sections of cables. Since the Adventure Cables cross the stitches within the stitch pattern and cross the stitch pattern stitches over the mitten, they sit higher up from the base mitten fabric, creating a deep level of texture. They remind me of canoeing along the edge of the very deep and crystal clear lake my mother-in-law lives beside. Looking down just feet from the shore, you can see the cliff face of the drop-off under the water and all the levels of rock below the surface.

Finished Size

Small (Medium, Large)
7½ (8½, 9) in./16 (21.5, 23) cm hand circumference and 7 (8¼, 9½) in./18 (21, 24) cm long from wrist to tip, 9½ (11, 12) in./24 (28, 30.5) cm total length including cuff; hand length is adjustable

Mittens shown measure 8½ in./21.5 cm in hand circumference.

Yarn

Berroco Ultra Alpaca (#4 medium weight; 50% super fine alpaca, 50% Peruvian wool; 219 yd./200 m per 3.5 oz./100 g): 1 skein #6285 Oceanic Mix

Needles

US size 5 (3.75 mm) set of double-pointed needles (dpns). Adjust needle size if necessary to obtain the correct gauge.

Notions

2 markers (m), cable needle (cn) optional, stitch holders, tapestry needle

Gauge

19 sts and 32 rows = 4 in./10 cm in stockinette stitch

24 sts = 3¼ in./8.5 cm in Adventure Cables Pattern, after blocking

Be Brave level/Experienced: This pattern has intricate patterning on the Adventure Cable such as crossed stitches or stranded colorwork stitches.

Pattern Notes

These mittens are worked from the bottom up in the round. 1/1 cables are worked during the Adventure Cables for an extra deeply textured cable pattern. During decreases in the front, stitches are initially decreased within the cable pattern; then they switch to decreases that absorb the remaining cable pattern. These mittens benefit from a wet blocking to open up the cable pattern and set the size.

Stitch Guide

2/2 RC with cn: Slip 2 sts to cn and hold in back, k2, k2 from cn.

2/2 RC without cn: Reach right needle tip in front of work and insert into the 3rd and 4th sts from left tip, slide all 4 sts off left tip, reinsert left tip into first 2 sts behind work, slide 2 sts from right tip back to left tip, k4.

1/1RT: Insert right tip into 2 sts as if to k2tog, wrap and pull through, do not drop off left needle; insert right tip into back of 1st st on left tip, wrap and pull through, drop all sts off left needle.

1/1LT: Insert right needle into back of 2nd st on left tip, wrap and pull through, do not drop off left tip; insert right tip into front of 1st st on left tip as if to knit, wrap and pull through, drop both sts off left needle.

Adventure Cables Stitch Guide
With Cable Needle

AC1: 4/2 RT, LT/K2 RC using cn: Slip 2 sts to cn and hold in back, 1/1 RT, 1/1 LT, and then k2 from cn.

AC2: 4/2 K2/RT, LT LC using cn: Slip 4 sts to cn and hold in front, p2, and then 1/1 RT, 1/1 LT from cn.

AC3: 4/2 RT, LT/P2 RC using cn: Slip 2 sts to cn and hold in back, 1/1 RT, 1/1 LT, and then p2 from cn.

AC4: 4/2 P2/RT, LT LC using cn: Slip 4 sts to cn and hold in front, p2, and then 1/1 RT, 1/1 LT from cn.

Without Cable Needle

AC1: 4/2 RT, LT/K2 RC without cn: Reach right needle tip in front of work and insert into the 3rd, 4th, 5th, and 6th sts from left tip, slide all 6 sts off left tip, reinsert left tip into first 2 sts behind work, slide 4 sts from right tip back to left tip, 1/1 RT, 1/1 LT, k2.

AC2: 4/2 K2/RT, LT LC without cn: Reach right needle tip behind work and insert into the 5th and 6th sts from left tip, slide all 6 sts off left tip, reinsert left tip into first 4 sts in front of work, slide 2 sts from right tip back to left tip, k2, 1/1 RT, 1/1 LT.

AC3: 4/2 RT, LT/P2 RC without cn: Reach right needle tip in front of work and insert into the 3rd, 4th, 5th, and 6th sts from left tip, slide all 6 sts off left tip, reinsert left tip into first 2 sts behind work, slide 4 sts from right tip back to left tip, 1/1 RT, 1/1 LT, p2.

AC4: 4/2 K2/RT, LT LC without cn: Reach right needle tip behind work and insert into the 5th and 6th sts from left tip, slide all 6 sts off left tip, reinsert left tip into first 4 sts in front of work, slide 2 sts from right tip back to left tip, p2, 1/1 RT, 1/1 LT.

INSTRUCTIONS

Cuff

CO 44 (48, 52) sts using the Old Norwegian method (*see Tutorial on page 39*) or an equally stretchy method. Join to work in the rnd, and pm to indicate beg of rnd.

Rnd 1: K0 (1, 2), *p2, k2; rep from * to last 0 (3, 2) sts, p0 (2, 2), k0 (1, 0).

Rep Rnd 1 until piece measures 2 (2½, 2¾) in./5 (6.5, 7) cm from cast-on edge.

Next Rnd: K1 (2, 3), p1, k2, p5, k8, p5, k2, p1, k1 (2, 3) pm, knit to end of rnd.

Body

Size Small only: K1, work Adventure Cable Chart to 1 st before m, k1, sm, knit to end of

rnd. Rep last rnd 3 more times, progressing through Rnds 2–4 of Adventure Cables Chart.

All Sizes

Right Hand Gusset Placement Rnd: K1 (2, 3), work Adventure Cable Pattern, k1 (2, 3), sm, M1L, pm, knit to end of rnd—45 (49, 53) sts.

Next Rnd: Work 1 rnd even progressing through Adventure Cable Pattern and knitting all other sts.

Inc Rnd: K1 (2, 3), work Adventure Cable Pattern, k1 (2, 3), sm, M1R, knit to m, M1L, sm, knit to end of rnd—47 (51, 55) sts.

Rep Inc Rnd every 3 (3, 2) rnds 5 (6, 7) more times—13 (15, 17) sts for gusset between markers, 57 (63, 69) sts total.

Work even if necessary to 2¾ (3, 3¼) in./7 (7.5, 8.25) cm from Gusset Placement Round.

Next Rnd: Work to m, sm, place foll 13 (15, 17) sts onto a holder or waste yarn, CO 1 st using the Backward Loop Method, remove m, knit to end—45 (49, 53) sts.

Work 2 rnds even progressing through Adventure Cable Pattern and knitting all other sts.

Dec Rnd: Work to m, sm, k2tog, knit to end of rnd—44 (48, 52) sts.

Work even progressing through Adventure Cable Pattern and knitting all other sts until piece measures 5½ (6½, 7½) in./14 (16.5, 19) cm from Gusset Placement Rnd or 1½ (1¾, 2) in./4 (4.5, 5) cm less than desired length.

At Same Time
After working Rows 1–24 of Adventure Cables Chart twice, work Rows 25–28 once, and then repeat Rows 29–32 as many times as needed for remainder of mitten—40 (44, 48) sts.

Roxboro Mittens Adventure Cable Chart

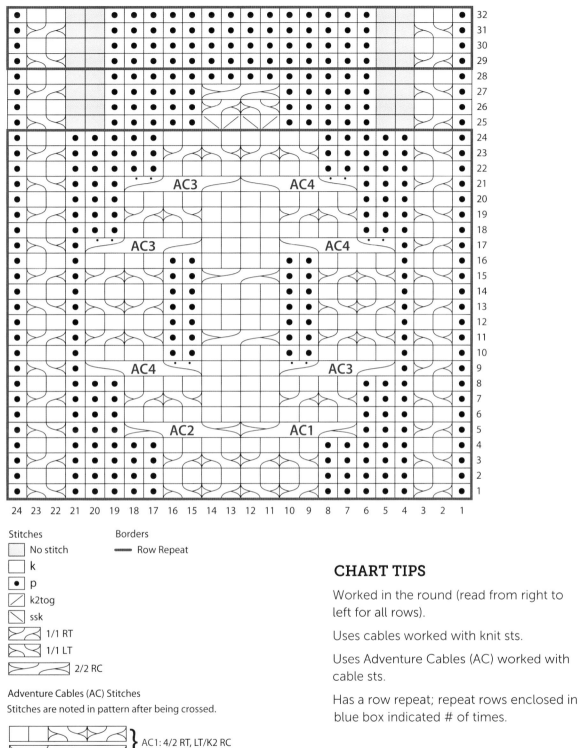

Stitches

- ▨ No stitch
- ☐ k
- ● p
- ⟋ k2tog
- ⟍ ssk
- 1/1 RT
- 1/1 LT
- 2/2 RC

Borders

- ▬▬ Row Repeat

Adventure Cables (AC) Stitches
Stitches are noted in pattern after being crossed.

AC1: 4/2 RT, LT/K2 RC

AC2: 4/2 K2/RT, LT LC

AC3: 4/2 RT, LT/P2 RC

AC4: 4/2 P2/RT, LT LC

CHART TIPS

Worked in the round (read from right to left for all rows).

Uses cables worked with knit sts.

Uses Adventure Cables (AC) worked with cable sts.

Has a row repeat; repeat rows enclosed in blue box indicated # of times.

Decreases

Initial Dec Rnd: K 1 (2, 3), work 3 sts in patt, p2tog, purl to 6 (7, 8) sts before m, p2tog, work sts in patt to m, sm, knit to end of rnd—2 sts dec'd.

Dec Rnd 1: K1 (2, 3), work 3 sts in patt, p2tog, purl to 6 (7, 8) sts before m, p2tog, work 3 sts in patt to m, sm, ssk, knit to 2 sts before end of rnd, k2tog.

Rep Dec Rnd 1 every rnd 5 more times—14 (18, 22) sts.

Dec Rnd 2: K1 (2, 3), p1, k1, ssk, k2tog, k1, p1, k1 (2, 3), sm, ssk, knit to 2 sts before end of rnd, k2tog—10 (14, 18) sts.

Dec Rnd 3: K1, ssk, knit to 3 sts before m, k2tog, k1, sm, ssk, knit to 2 sts before end of rnd, k2tog—6 (10, 14) sts.

Sizes Medium (Large) only: Rep Dec Rnd 3: 1 (2) more times—6 sts.

Cut yarn leaving a 6 in./15 cm tail, thread through remaining sts using a tapestry needle, pull tight and weave in end.

Work Left Mitten same as first, substituting Left Hand Gusset section as follows:

Left Hand Gusset Placement Rnd: K1 (2, 3), work Adventure Cable Pattern, k 1 (2, 3), sm, knit to end of rnd, pm, M1L, sm—45 (49, 53) sts.

Next Rnd: Work 1 rnd even progressing through Adventure Cable Pattern and knitting all other sts.

Inc Rnd: K1 (2, 3), work Adventure Cables Pattern, k1 (2, 3), sm, knit to m, sm, M1R, knit to m, M1L, sm—47 (51, 55) sts.

Rep Inc Rnd every 3 (3, 2) rnds 5 (6, 7) more times—13 (15, 17) sts for gusset between markers, 57 (63, 69) sts total.

Work even if necessary to 2¾ (3, 3¼) in./7 (7.5, 8.5) cm from Gusset Placement Round.

Next Rnd: Work to m, sm, knit to m, remove marker, place foll 13 (15, 17) sts onto a holder or waste yarn, CO 1 st using the Backward Loop Method, sm—45 (49, 53) sts.

Work 2 rnds even progressing through Adventure Cables Pattern and knitting all other sts.

Dec Rnd: Work to m, sm, knit to 2 sts before end of rnd, ssk, sm—44 (48, 52) sts.

Work even progressing through Adventure Cables Pattern and knitting all other sts until piece measures 5½ (6½, 7½) in./14 (16.5, 19) cm from Gusset Placement Rnd or 1½ (1¾, 2) in./4 (4.5, 5) cm less than desired length. Work Decreases the same as Right mitten.

Thumb

Place 13 (15, 17) sts onto dpns, beg at gap pick up and knit 3 sts, knit around sts on needles, join to work in the round and place m to indicate beg of rnd—16 (18, 20) sts.

Work even in stockinette until thumb measures 1¾ (2, 2) in./4.5 (5, 5) cm from pickup rnd.

Dec Rnd: *K2tog; rep from * around—8 (9, 10) sts.

Knit 1 rnd.

Dec Rnd: K 0 (1, 0), *k2tog; rep from * around—4 (5, 5) sts.

Cut yarn leaving a 6 in./15 cm tail, thread through rem sts using a tapestry needle, pull tight, and weave in end.

Repeat for second thumb.

Finishing

Weave in any loose ends; wet block mittens to set shape and size.

Goose Prairie Vest

Worked from the bottom up all in one piece, this vest has simple shaping to complement the ornate Adventure Cables Pattern. A truly cabled cable, this pattern has one stitch crossing over three-stitch cables that twist around sections of stockinette, edging the front of this long vest. The back is worked in a purl ridge texture pattern to add interest and highlight the beautiful color variation of the hand-dyed yarn.

This stitch pattern was hands-down the most difficult stitch pattern to design in the whole book, and I redid it at least eight times. Getting the perfect balance between a cabled Adventure Cable crossing, a stitch pattern that looked different from just a regular cable pattern, and not adding too many elements into it all was difficult, although I am thrilled with the final product. It reminds me of a long drive we took when I was young: We were traveling across the prairie in the middle of the long, drawn-out twilight that is a Canadian summer. The moon was visible in the sky on one side of the car while the sun was setting on the other, and the range of blue in the sky and unending wheat fields all around was stunning.

Be Brave level/Experienced: This pattern has intricate patterning on the Adventure Cable such as crossed stitches or stranded colorwork stitches.

Finished Sizes
32 (36¼, 40¼, 44¼, 48½) (52½, 55½, 59¾, 63¾, 68) in./81.5 (92, 102, 112.5, 123) (133.5, 141, 152, 162, 172.5) cm

Shown in size 40¼ in./102 cm bust, modeled with 4 in./0.5 cm of positive ease.

Yarn
Sweet Georgia Yarns Superwash DK (#4 medium weight; 100% superwash merino; 256 yd./234 m per 4 oz./115 g): 4 (4, 4, 5, 5) (5, 6, 6, 7, 7) skeins Deep Cove

Needles
US sizes 4 (3.5 mm) and 6 (4.0 mm): 32 in./81 cm circular needle

US size 4 (3.5 mm): double-pointed needles (dpns) and 16 in./41 cm circular needle (optional for larger size armhole edgings)

Adjust needle size if necessary to obtain the correct gauge.

Notions
6 stitch markers (m), 6 removable stitch markers, two cable needles (cn) optional, tapestry needle

Gauge
20 sts and 27½ rows = 4 in./10 cm in Stockinette st

19 sts and 30 rows = 4 in./10 cm in Back Texture Pattern

32 sts = 4¾ in./12 cm over Adventure Cables Pattern, lightly steam blocked

Pattern Notes

This vest is worked flat, knit back and forth all in one piece. Decreases are worked on the lower body to create an A-line shape, while the upper body is worked straight for a casual look. Since the upper fronts are worked without decreases to the neck, the shoulder seam for this garment sits behind the neck. The armholes for the vest are worked with ribbing, but sleeves could be added easily. When designing this pattern, it became clear that crossing the cabled stitches in front of the knit stitches required an Adventure Cable, but crossing the knit stitches in front of the cabled stitches looked the same as crossing the knit stitches over knit stitches. For this reason, there are only 4 Adventure Cables in this pattern. It is easiest to work these cables without a cable needle, but instructions have been provided for both methods. When working with the hand-dyed yarn, it is best practice to work with 2 skeins at the same time and alternate skeins every 2 rows.

Alteration Information

Note: Any alterations made may affect yardage amounts used.

✳ The body length of this garment can be adjusted by adding or removing length before the armhole division. If you are removing 1–2 inches of length, then decrease the number of rows worked even between decreases to 16. If you are removing 3–4 inches, then decrease the number of rows worked between decreases to 14.

✳ Sleeves can easily be added to this vest; see the sleeve alteration instructions on page 19. The armholes for this vest are the same depth as the Point Defiance Pullover, so a sleeve can be selected from that pattern if desired.

Stitch Guide

3/3 RC with cn: Slip 3 sts to cn and hold in back, k3, k3 from cn.

3/3 LC with cn: Slip 3 sts to cn and hold in front, k3, k3 from cn.

2/4 RC with cn: Slip 4 sts to cn and hold in back, k4, k2 from cn.

2/4 LC with cn: Slip 2 sts to cn and hold in front, k4, k2 from cn.

3/3 RC without cn: Reach right tip in front of work and insert into the 4th, 5th, and 6th sts from left tip, slide 6 sts off left tip, reinsert left tip into first 3 sts behind work, slide 3 sts from right tip to left tip, k6.

3/3 LC without cn: Reach right needle tip behind work and insert into the 4th, 5th, and 6th sts from left tip, slide 6 sts off left tip, reinsert left tip into first 3 sts in front of work, slide 3 sts from right tip back to left tip, k6.

2/4 RC without cn: Reach right tip in front of work and insert into the 5th and 6th sts from left tip, slide 6 sts off left tip, reinsert left tip into first 4 sts behind work, slide 2 sts from right tip to left tip, k6.

2/4 LC without cn: Reach right needle tip behind work and insert into the 3rd, 4th, 5th, and 6th sts from left tip, slide 6 sts off left tip, reinsert left tip into first 2 sts in front of work, slide 4 sts from right tip back to left tip, k6.

1/1 RT: Insert right tip into 2 sts as if to k2tog, wrap and pull through, do not drop off left needle; insert right tip into back of 1st st on left tip, wrap and pull through; drop all sts off left needle.

1/1 LT: Insert right needle into back of 2nd st on left tip, wrap and pull through, do not drop off left tip; insert right tip into front of 1st st on left tip, wrap and pull through; drop both sts off left needle.

Adventure Cables Stitch Guide
With Cable Needles
AC1: 3/3 K3/1OVER2 LC with cn: Slip 3 sts to cn and hold in front, k3, slip 1st st on cn onto 2nd cn and hold in front, k2 from 1st cn, k1 from 2nd cn.

AC2: 3/3 1OVER2/K3 RC with cn: Slip 3 st to cn and hold in back, slip next 2 sts onto 2nd cn and hold in back, k1, k2 from 2nd cn, k3 from 1st cn.

AC3: 4/2 RT, LT/K2 RC with cn: Slip 2 sts to cn and hold in back, 1/1 RT, 1/1 LT, and then k2 from cn.

AC4: 4/2 K2/RT, LT LC with cn: Slip 4 sts to cn and hold in front, k2 then 1/1 RT, 1/1 LT from cn.

Without Cable Needle
AC1: 3/3 K3/1OVER2 LC without cn: Reach right needle tip behind work and insert into the 4th, 5th, and 6th sts from left tip, slide all 6 sts off left tip, reinsert left tip into first 3

sts in front of work, slide 3 sts from right tip back to left tip, k3. Bring right needle behind work and insert into the 2nd and 3rd sts from tip, slide 3 sts off left tip, reinsert left tip into 1st st in front of work, slide 2 sts from right tip back to left tip, k3. *See Photo Tutorial on page 130.*

AC2: 3/3 1OVER2/K3 RC without cn: Reach right needle tip in front of work and insert into the 4th, 5th, and 6th sts from left tip, slide all 6 sts off left tip, reinsert left tip into first 3 sts behind work, slide 3 sts from right tip back to left tip. Reach right needle tip in front of work and insert into the 3rd st from left tip, slide all 3 sts off left tip, reinsert left tip into first 2 sts behind work, slide 1 st from right tip back to left tip, k6. *See Photo Tutorial on page 132.*

AC3: 4/2 RT, LT/K2 RC without cn: Reach right needle tip in front of work and insert into the 3rd, 4th, 5th, and 6th sts from left tip, slide all 6 sts off left tip, reinsert left tip into first 2 sts behind work, slide 4 sts from right tip back to left tip, 1/1 RT, 1/1 LT, k2.

AC4: 4/2 K2/RT, LT LC without cn: Reach right needle tip behind work and insert into the 5th and 6th sts from left tip, slide all 6 sts off left tip, reinsert left tip into 1st 4 sts in front of work, slide 2 sts from right tip back to left tip, k2, 1/1 RT, 1/1 LT.

Back Texture Pattern
Rows 1, 2, and 3: Knit across.

Row 4: Purl across.

Rep these 4 rows for patt.

INSTRUCTIONS

Lower Body

Using smaller 32 in./81 cm needles, CO 192 (212, 232, 252, 272) (292, 307, 327, 347, 367) sts.

Setup Row (RS): K5, pm, [p2, k2] 2 times, p2, k3, p2, k2, p2, k3, [p2, k2] 2 times, p2, pm, *k3, p2; rep from * to last 40 sts, k3, pm, [p2, k2] 2 times, p2, k3, p2, k2, p2, k3, [p2, k2] 2 times, p2, pm, k5.

Next Row (WS): K5, sm, [k2, p2] 2 times, k2, p3, k2, p2, k2, p3, [k2, p2] 2 times, k2, sm, *p3, k2; rep from * to 3 sts before marker, p3, sm, [k2, p2] 2 times, k2, p3, k2, p2, k2, p3, [k2, p2] 2 times, k2, sm, k5.

Cont in patt as est slipping markers for 6 more rows.

Change to larger 32 in./81 cm circular needles.

Pattern Setup Row (RS): K5, sm, work Adventure Cables Chart to m, sm, k15 (20, 25, 30, 35) (40, 45, 50, 55, 60), pm for side shaping, work Back Texture Pattern over next 88 (98, 108, 118, 128) (138, 143, 153, 163, 173) sts, pm for side shaping, knit to m, sm, work Adventure Cables Chart to m, sm, k5.

Next Row (WS): K5, sm, work Adventure Cables Chart to m, sm, purl to m, sm, work Back Texture Pattern to m, sm, purl to m, sm, work Adventure Cables Chart to m, sm, k5.

Goose Prairie Vest Adventure Cables Chart

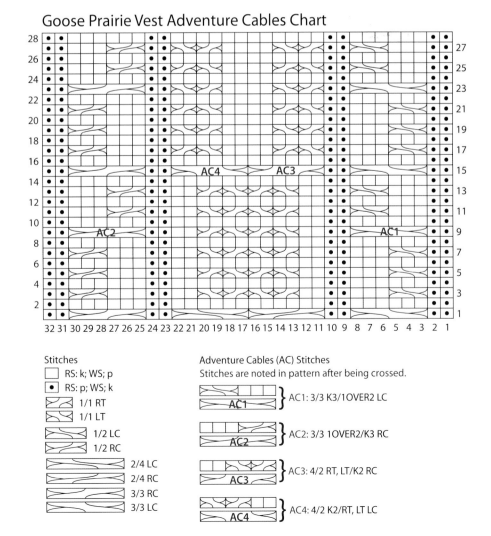

CHART TIPS

Worked flat (read from right to left for RS rows, left to right for WS rows).

Uses cables worked with knit sts.

Uses Adventure Cables (AC) worked with cable sts.

Chart rows are repeatable for pattern length adjustment.

Cont in patt as est, working first and last 5 sts as garter, progressing through Adventure Cables Chart, working sts between side shaping markers in Back Texture Pattern, and working all other sts as stockinette for 18 more rows, ending with a WS row.

Dec Row (RS): [Work in patt as est to 3 sts before side shaping marker, ssk, k1, sm, k1, k2tog] twice, work in patt to end—4 sts decreased.

Rep Dec Row every 22 rows 4 more times—172 (192, 212, 232, 252) (272, 287, 307, 327, 347) sts.

Cont in patt as est, working first and last 5 sts as garter, progressing through Adventure Cables Chart, working sts between side shaping markers in Back Texture Pattern, and working all other sts as stockinette until

piece measures 18 in./45.5 cm. Place removable markers around the first and last sts.

Divide for Armholes
Right Front
Row 1 (RS): Work to side shaping marker in patt as est, turn work, remove marker. Place rem back sts and left front sts onto a holder or waste yarn—47 (52, 57, 62, 67) (72, 77, 82, 87, 92) sts rem on needle for right front.

Row 2 (WS): K1, work to end in patt as est.

Cont in patt as est, working first 5 sts and last 1 st as garter, progressing through Adventure Cables Chart, and working all other sts as stockinette until piece measures 6¾ (7, 7½, 8¼, 9¼) (10, 10¾, 11, 11¼, 11½) in./17 (18, 19, 21, 23.5) (25.5, 27.5, 28, 28.5, 29) cm from armhole division ending with a WS row.

Sizes 32 (36¼, 40¼, 44¼, 48½) (52½) in./81 (92, 102, 112, 123) (133) cm only

Dec Row: K5, [p2, k1, k2tog, k1, k2tog] twice, [ssk, k1, ssk, k1, p2] twice, remove marker, knit to end—39 (44, 49, 54, 59) (64) sts. BO all sts on WS row.

Sizes 55½ (59¾, 63¾, 68) in./141 (152, 162, 173) cm only

Dec Row: K5, [p2, k1, k2tog, k1, k2tog] twice, [ssk, k1, ssk, k1, p2] twice, remove marker, [k11 (13, 14, 16) k2tog] 3 times, k1 (0, 2, 1)—66 (71, 76, 81) sts. BO all sts on WS row.

Back

Reattach yarn to work across RS of rem sts.

Row 1 (RS): Work Back Texture Pattern to side shaping marker, remove marker, turn work. Place rem 47 (52, 57, 62, 67) (72, 77, 82, 87, 92) sts for Left Front onto a stitch holder or waste yarn.

Cont in Back Texture Pattern until piece measures 6¾ (7, 7½, 8¼, 9¼) (10, 10¾, 11, 11¼, 11½) in./17 (18, 19, 21, 23.5) (25.5, 27.5, 28, 28.5, 29.25) cm from armhole division ending with a WS row. BO all sts.

Left Front

Reattach yarn to work across RS of rem sts.

Cont in patt as est, working first 1 st and last 5 sts as garter, progressing through Adventure Cables Chart, and working all other sts as stockinette until piece measures 6¾ (7, 7½, 8¼, 9¼) (10, 10¾, 11, 11¼, 11½) in./17 (17.75, 19, 21, 23.5) (25, 27.25, 28, 28.5, 29.25) cm from armhole division ending with a WS row.

Sizes 32 (36¼, 40¼, 44¼, 48½) (52½) in./81 (92, 102, 112, 123) (133) cm only

Dec Row: Knit to m, sm, [p2, k1, k2tog, k1, k2tog] twice, [ssk, k1, ssk, k1, p2] twice, remove marker, k5—39 (44, 49, 54, 59) (64) sts. BO all sts on WS row.

Sizes 55½ (59¾, 63¾, 68) in./141 (152, 162, 173) cm only

Dec Row: K1 (0, 2, 1), [k11 (13, 14, 16) k2tog] 3 times, sm, [p2, k1, k2tog, k1, k2tog] twice, [ssk, k1, ssk, k1, p2] twice, remove marker, k5—66 (71, 76, 81) sts. BO all sts on WS row.

Seaming

Using tapestry needle, seam Fronts to Back at shoulders.

Armhole Edgings

Using US size 3 (3.5 mm) dpns or 16 in./41 cm circular needle, pick up and knit 65 (70, 75, 85, 95) (100, 105, 110, 115, 120) sts evenly around armhole (see tip on this technique on page 21). Join to work in the round and pm (place marker) for beg of rnd.

Rnd 1: *K3, p2; rep from * around.

Rep this rnd 3 more times. BO all sts.

Finishing

Work in any loose ends and steam block lightly to set patt.

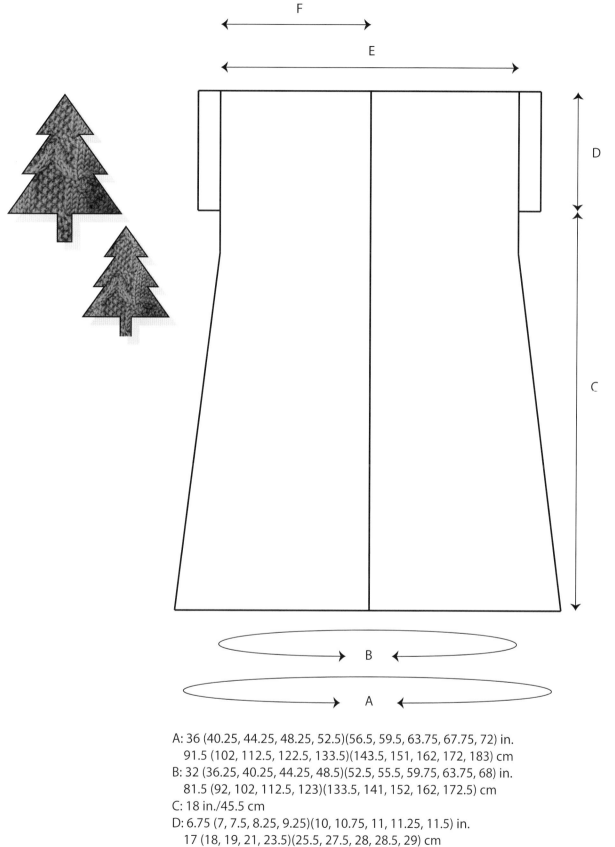

A: 36 (40.25, 44.25, 48.25, 52.5)(56.5, 59.5, 63.75, 67.75, 72) in.
   91.5 (102, 112.5, 122.5, 133.5)(143.5, 151, 162, 172, 183) cm
B: 32 (36.25, 40.25, 44.25, 48.5)(52.5, 55.5, 59.75, 63.75, 68) in.
   81.5 (92, 102, 112.5, 123)(133.5, 141, 152, 162, 172.5) cm
C: 18 in./45.5 cm
D: 6.75 (7, 7.5, 8.25, 9.25)(10, 10.75, 11, 11.25, 11.5) in.
   17 (18, 19, 21, 23.5)(25.5, 27.5, 28, 28.5, 29) cm
E: 16.5 (18.5, 20.75, 22.75, 24.75)(27, 28, 30, 32.25, 34.25) in.
   42 (47, 52.5, 58, 63)(68.5, 71, 76, 82, 87) cm
F: 7.75 (8.75, 9.75, 10.75, 11.75)(12.75, 13.25, 14.25, 15.25, 16.25) in.
   19.5 (22, 25, 27.5, 30)(32.5, 33.5, 36, 38.5, 41.5) cm

TUTORIAL: How to Work the AC1 and AC2

The Goose Prairie Vest uses crossings that have cabled stitches worked within the Adventure Cables. These Adventure Cables are 1 over 2 cables that then cross over a 3-stitch section of stockinette and leave a beautifully ornate cable with extra texture and movement. It is possible to work these Adventure Cables with a cable needle, but it is easier to work them without since there are two crossings worked at the same time, and you will require two cable needles. The following tutorial shows how to work both crossings without a cable needle by first rearranging the 6 stitches used for the entire Adventure Cable and then moving a single stitch over 2 stitches within the Adventure Cable.

 On the chart, both AC1 and AC2 are noted over 6 sts; the 1/3 cable patterning continues over the 3 sts that received this patterning on the previous right-side rows. The 1/3 cable patterning crosses in front of the knit stitches for both the AC1 and the AC2. AC1 is a left-leaning cross and AC2 is a right-leaning cross. The cable patterning is only worked on the Adventure Cables where the cable patterning crosses in front of the stockinette stitches; there was no visual difference when the cable patterning was continued behind the stockinette stitches, so those cables are worked as a regular 3/3 cross.

ADVENTURE CABLE 1: AC1

1. On Row 9, work through stitch 2 (stitch 2 is completed as a purl stitch and is located on the right-hand needle; stitch 3 is on the left-hand needle waiting to be worked).

2. Reach right needle behind the work and insert into the 4th, 5th, and 6th sts from needle tip.

3. Slip all 6 sts off the left tip. The 1st, 2nd, and 3rd sts are now loose in front of the work.

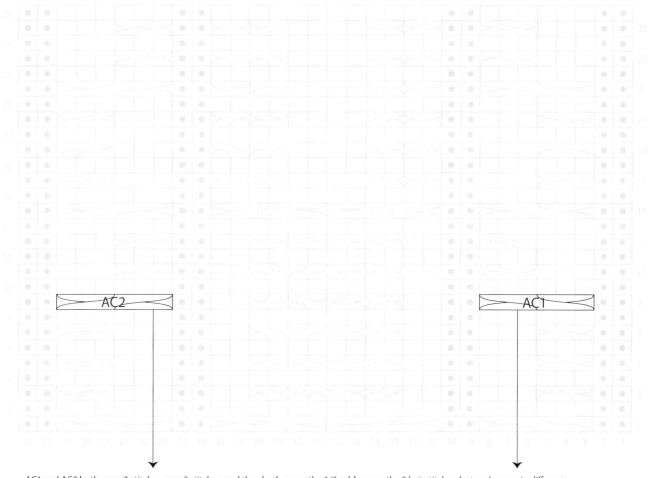

AC1 and AC2 both cross 3 stitches over 3 stitches, and they both move the 1/3 cables over the 3 knit stitches, but each move in different directions. It is possible to use two cable needles to complete these Adventure Cables, but it is simpler to work them without a cable needle as shown here.

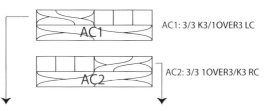

AC1: 3/3 K3/1OVER3 LC

AC2: 3/3 1OVER3/K3 RC

Both AC1 and AC2 continue the 1/3 cable during the Adventure Cable, as can be seen on the Adventure Cables key.

4. Bring the left needle to the front of the work and slip the 1st, 2nd, and 3rd sts onto it.

5. Slip the 3 sts from the right tip to the left tip.

6. Knit the first 3 sts.

7. Reach the right needle behind the work again and insert it into the 2nd and 3rd sts from the left tip.

8. Slip the first 3 sts off the left tip, the 1st st is now loose in front of the work.

9. Reach the left needle tip in front of the work and insert into the loose stitch.

10. Slip the 2 sts from the right tip to the left tip.

11. Knit these final 3 sts.

ADVENTURE CABLE 2: AC2

1. On Row 9, work through stitch 24 (stitch 24 is completed as a purl stitch and is located on the right-hand needle; stitch 25 is on the left-hand needle waiting to be worked.

2. Reach right needle in front of the work and insert into the 4th, 5th, and 6th sts from needle tip.

3. Slip all 6 sts off the left tip. The 1st, 2nd, and 3rd sts are now loose behind the work.

4. Bring the left needle behind the work and slip the 1st, 2nd, and 3rd sts onto it.

5. Slip the 3 sts from the right tip to the left tip.

6. Reach the right needle in front of the work and insert into the 3rd st.

7. Slip the first 3 sts off the left tip. The 1st and 2nd sts are now loose behind the work.

8. Insert the left tip into the 2 loose sts behind the work.

9. Slip the single stitch from the right tip to the left tip.

10. Knit across the rearranged 6 sts.

Seven Bays Cardigan

Worked from the bottom up in pieces, this cardigan has cabled Adventure Cables crossed over more traditional cables and crisp vertical lines of twisted knit stitches. The wide front bands of patterning are continued up the front and around the back neck and are edged with a double knit trim. This longer length cardigan has slight A-line shaping and drop sleeves for a comfy and casual look.

I knew that I wanted to include in this book a really classic cardigan with no fasteners, and I wanted to play with what would be thought of as traditional cables, but with added Adventure Cables texture. The resulting stitch pattern has great flow since the right and left twists are simple to work, enhancing the cables with added texture for not much extra work. The lines of textured stitches look like tiny tracks in the sand by a river or lake. Perhaps a small creature has skittered across, leaving a strangely geometric pattern behind before a gently lapping wave smooths it away.

Be Brave level/Experienced: This pattern has intricate patterning on the Adventure Cable such as crossed stitches or stranded colorwork stitches.

Finished Sizes
36½ (39¾, 42¾, 47½, 50½) (54, 60¼, 63¼, 66¼, 71) in./ 92.5 (101, 108.5, 120.5, 128.5) (137, 153, 160.5, 168.5, 180.5) cm bust circumference

Shown in size 42¾ in./108.5 cm, modeled with 3¼ in./8.5 cm of positive ease.

Yarn
Sweet Georgia Yarns Superwash DK (#4 medium weight; 100% superwash merino; 256 yd./234 m per 4 oz./115 g): 6 (6, 7, 7, 8) (9, 9, 10, 10, 11) skeins Tumbled Stone

Needles
US sizes 4 (3.5 mm) and 6 (4.0 mm): 24 in./61 cm circular or straight needles, and double-pointed needles (dpns)

US size 6 (4.0 mm): 16 in./41 cm circular needle (optional for larger size sleeves)

Adjust needle size if necessary to obtain the correct gauge.

Notions
2 stitch markers (m), 4 removable stitch markers, cable needle (cn) optional, tapestry needle

Gauge
20½ sts and 26 rows = 4 in./10 cm in stockinette

62 sts = 9¼ in./23.5 cm over Adventure Cables Back Chart Pattern, lightly steam blocked

3½ in./9 cm = 29 sts—26 sts of Adventure Cables Left Front Chart Pattern and 3 double knit edge sts

Pattern Notes

This cardigan is worked back and forth from the bottom up in pieces. Since this is a longer cardigan worked in superwash yarn, the side seams give the cardigan structure and prevent it from stretching. When working with the hand-dyed yarn, it is best practice to work with 2 skeins at the same time and alternate skeins every 2 rows. For the left front, alternate skeins at the beginning of the RS row; for the right front, alternate skeins at the beginning of the WS row.

Alteration Information

Note: Any alterations made may affect yardage amounts used.

- ✳ The body length of this garment can be adjusted by adding or removing length before the armhole division. If you are removing 1–2 inches of length, then decrease the number of rows worked even between decreases to 18. If you are removing 3–4 inches, then decrease the number of rows worked between decreases to 16.
- ✳ Sleeve length can be adjusted by removing or adding rounds worked even before decreases. If a wider cuff is desired, remove decreases in sets of 2 so the cuff rib patt will still have a multiple of 4 sts in the final count.
- ✳ Upper-arm circumference and armhole depth can be altered by using the sleeve alteration instructions on page 19.
- ✳ Need extra front coverage? Choose one size larger when creating the left and right fronts; the majority of the sizes are only 4 stitches different. A little math: Add the *stitch difference* between the initial size and the substituted size to the already calculated front decreases of 1 (1, 1, 1, 1) (1, 3, 3, 4, 2) = **total needed front decrease**.

Take your armhole depth, multiply it by your rows per inch, and then divide that number by your new **total needed front decrease**. Round this to the closest even number and work that many rows in between your new number of decreases.

Stitch Guide

Rib (multiple of 4)
Rnd 1: K1, *p2, k2; rep from * to last 3 sts, p2, k1.

Rep Rnd 1 for patt.

2/2 RC with cn: Slip 2 sts to cn and hold in back, k2, k2 from cn.

2/2 LC with cn: Slip 2 sts to cn and hold in front, k2, k2 from cn.

2/2 RC without cn: Reach right tip in front of work and insert into the 3rd and 4th sts from left tip, slide 4 sts off left tip, reinsert left tip into first 2 sts behind work, slide 2 sts from right tip to left tip, k4.

2/2 LC without cn: Reach right needle tip behind work and insert into the 3rd and 4th sts from left tip, slide 4 sts off left tip, reinsert left tip into first 2 sts in front of work, slide 2 sts from right tip back to left tip, k4.

1/1 RT: Insert right tip into 2 sts as if to k2tog, wrap and pull through, do not drop off left needle; insert right tip into back of 1st st on left tip, wrap and pull through, drop all sts off left needle.

1/1 LT: Insert right needle into back of 2nd st on left tip, wrap and pull through, do not drop off left tip; insert right tip into front of 1st stitch on left tip as if to knit, wrap and pull through, drop both sts off left needle.

Adventure Cables Stitch Guide
With Cable Needle
AC1: 4/1 P1/RT, LT LC with cn: Slip 4 sts to cn and hold in front, p1, and then 1/1 RT, 1/1 LT from cn.

AC2: 4/1 RT, LT/P1 RC with cn: Slip 1 st to cn and hold in back, 1/1 RT, 1/1 LT, and then p1 from cn.

AC3: 4/4 K4/RT, LT LC with cn: Slip 4 sts to cn and hold in front, k4, and then 1/1 RT, 1/1 LT from cn.

AC4: 4/4 RT, LT/K4 RC with cn: Slip 4 sts to cn and hold in back, 1/1 RT, 1/1 LT, and then k4 from cn.

AC5: 4/4 RT, LT/K4 LC with cn: Slip 4 sts to cn and hold in front, 1/1 RT, 1/1 LT, and then k4 from cn.

AC6: 4/4 K4/RT, LT RC with cn: Slip 4 sts to cn and hold in back, k4, and then 1/1 RT, 1/1 LT from cn.

Without Cable Needle
AC1: 4/1 P1/RT, LT LC without cn: Reach right needle tip behind work and insert into the 5th st from left tip, slide all 5 sts off left tip, reinsert left tip into first 4 sts in front of work, slide 1 st from right tip back to left tip, p1, 1/1 RT, 1/1 LT.

AC2: 4/1 RT, LT/P1 RC without cn: Reach right needle tip in front of work and insert into the 2nd, 3rd, 4th, and 5th sts from left tip, slide all 5 sts off left tip, reinsert left tip into 1st st behind work, slide 4 sts from right tip back to left tip, 1/1 RT, 1/1 LT, p1.

AC3: 4/4 K4/RT, LT LC without cn: Reach right needle tip behind work and insert into the 5th, 6th, 7th, and 8th sts from left tip, slide all 8 sts off left tip, reinsert left tip into first 4 sts in front of work, slide 4 sts from right tip back to left tip, k4, 1/1 RT, 1/1 LT.

AC4: 4/4 RT, LT/K4 RC without cn: Reach right needle tip in front of work and insert into the 5th, 6th, 7th, and 8th sts from left tip, slide all 8 sts off left tip, reinsert left tip into first 4 sts behind work, slide 4 sts from right tip back to left tip, 1/1 RT, 1/1 LT, k4.

AC5: 4/4 RT, LT/K4 LC without cn: Reach right needle tip behind work and insert into the 5th, 6th, 7th, and 8th sts from left tip, slide all 8 sts off left tip, reinsert left tip into first 4 sts in front of work, slide 4 sts from right tip back to left tip, 1/1 RT, 1/1 LT, k4.

AC6: 4/4 K4/RT, LT RC without cn: Reach right needle tip in front of work and insert into the 5th, 6th, 7th, and 8th sts from left tip, slide all 8 sts off left tip, reinsert left tip into first 4 sts behind work, slide 4 sts from right tip back to left tip, k4, 1/1 RT, 1/1 LT.

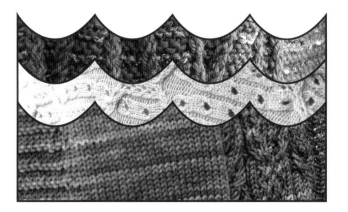

INSTRUCTIONS

Back

Using smaller 24 in./61 cm needles, CO 120 (128, 136, 152, 160) (168, 184, 192, 200, 216) sts.

Setup Row (RS): K1, [p2, k2] 7 (8, 9, 11, 12) (13, 15, 16, 17, 19) times, pm, p2, k1tbl, p2, k4, p2, k1tbl, p2 [k4, p2] 2 times, k1tbl, p2, k4, p2, k1tbl, [p2, k4] 2 times, p2, k1tbl, p2, k4, p2, k1tbl, p2, pm, [k2, p2] 7 (8, 9, 11, 12) (13, 15, 16, 17, 19) times, k1.

Next Row (WS): K1, *k2, p2; rep from * to marker, sm, k2, p1tbl, k2, p4, k2, p1tbl, k2, [p4, k2] 2 times, p1tbl, k2, p4, k2, p1tbl, [k2, p4] 2 times, k2, p1tbl, k2, p4, k2, p1tbl, k2, sm, *p2, k2; rep from * to last stitch, k1.

Cont in patt as est, slipping markers, for 6 more rows.

Change to larger 24 in./61 cm circular needles.

Pattern Setup Row (RS): Knit to m, sm, work Adventure Cables Back Chart to m, sm, knit to end.

Next Row (WS): K1, purl to m, sm, work Adventure Cables Back Chart to m, sm, purl to last stitch, k1.

Cont in patt as est, working first and last sts as garter, progressing through Adventure Cables Back Pattern between markers, and working all other sts as stockinette for 20 more rows, ending with a WS row.

Dec Row (RS): K1, k2tog, work in patt to last 3 sts, ssk, k1—2 sts decreased.

Rep Dec Row every 20 rows 4 more times—110 (118, 126, 142, 150) (158, 174, 182, 190, 206) sts.

Cont in patt as est, working first and last sts as garter, progressing through Adventure Cables Back Pattern between markers, and working all other sts as stockinette until piece measures 18 in./45.5 cm. Place removable markers around the first and last sts.

Seven Bays Cardigan Adventure Cables Back Chart

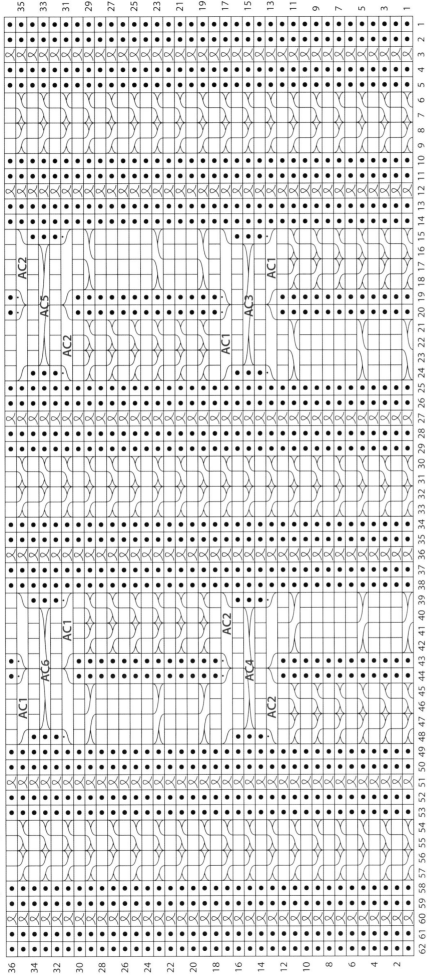

CHART TIPS

Worked flat (read from right to left for RS rows, left to right for WS rows).

Uses cables worked with knit sts.

Uses Adventure Cables (AC) worked with cable sts.

Chart rows are repeatable for pattern length adjustment.

AC5: 4/4 RT, LT/K4 LC

AC6: 4/4 K4/RT, LT RC

AC3: 4/4 K4/RT, LT LC

AC4: 4/4 RT, LT/K4 RC

Adventure Cables (AC) Stitches

Stitches are noted in pattern after being crossed.

AC1: 4/1 P1/RT, LT LC

AC2: 4/1 RT, LT/P1 RC

Stitches

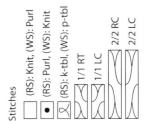

(RS): Knit, (WS): Purl

(RS): Purl, (WS): Knit

(RS): k-tbl, (WS): p-tbl

1/1 RT

1/1 LC

2/2 RC

2/2 LC

Armholes

Cont in patt as est, working first and last sts as garter, progressing through Adventure Cables Back Pattern between markers, and working all other sts as stockinette until piece measures 5¾ (6, 6½, 7¼, 8¼) (9, 9¾, 10, 10¼, 10½) in./14.5 (15, 16.5, 18.5, 21) (23, 25, 25.5, 26, 26.5) cm, ending with a WS row.

Neck Shaping: Work 32 (36, 40, 44, 48) (52, 58, 62, 65, 71) sts in patt, BO 46 (46, 46, 54, 54) (54, 58, 58, 60, 64) sts, work to end in patt—32 (36, 40, 44, 48) (52, 58, 62, 65, 71) sts each side.

Left Back

Dec Row (WS): Work to last 2 sts, p2tog tbl, turn work.

Dec Row (RS): Ssk, work to end.

Rep last 2 rows twice more—26 (30, 34, 38, 42) (46, 52, 56, 59, 65) sts.

Work even to 6¾ (7, 7½, 8¼, 9¼) (10, 10¾, 11, 11¼, 11½) in./17 (18, 19, 21, 23.5) (25.5, 27.5, 28, 28.5, 29) cm if necessary. BO all sts.

Right Back

Reattach yarn to work across WS.

Dec Row (WS): P2tog, work to end.

Dec Row (RS): Work to last 2 sts, k2tog.

Rep last 2 rows twice more—26 (30, 34, 38, 42) (46, 52, 56, 59, 65) sts.

Work even to 6¾ (7, 7½, 8¼, 9¼) (10, 10¾, 11, 11¼, 11½) in./17 (18, 19, 21, 23.5) (25.5, 27.5, 28, 28.5, 29) cm if necessary. BO all sts.

Left Front

Using smaller needles, CO 62 (66, 70, 74, 78) (82, 90, 94, 98, 102) sts.

Setup Row (RS): K1, [p2, k2] 8 (9, 10, 11, 12) (13, 15, 16, 17, 18) times, pm, [p2, k4] twice, p2, k1tbl, p2, k4, p2, k1tbl, p2, k1, sl1 wyif, k1.

Next Row (WS): Sl1 wyif, k1, sl1 wyif, k2, p1tbl, k2, p4, k2, p1tbl, k2, [p4, k2] twice, sm, *p2, k2; rep from * to last stitch, k1.

Cont in patt, slipping markers for 6 more rows.

Change to larger 32 in./81 cm circular needles.

Pattern Setup Row (RS): Knit to m, sm, work Adventure Cables Left Front Chart to last 3 sts, k1, sl1 wyif, k1.

Next Row (WS): Sl1 wyif, k1, sl1 wyif, work Adventure Cables Left Front Chart to m, sm, purl to last stitch, k1.

Seven Bays Cardigan Adventure Cables Left Front Chart

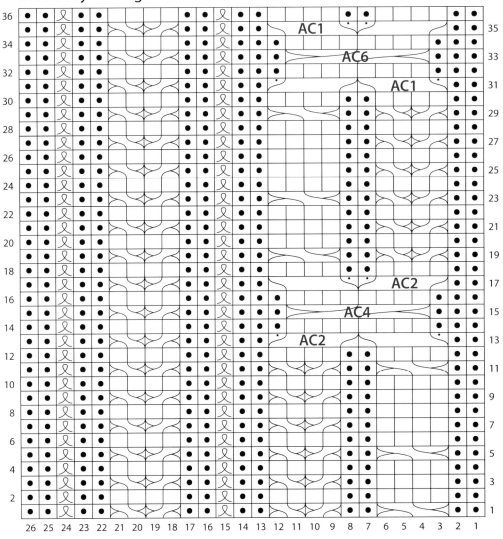

Seven Bays Cardigan Adventure Cables Right Front Chart

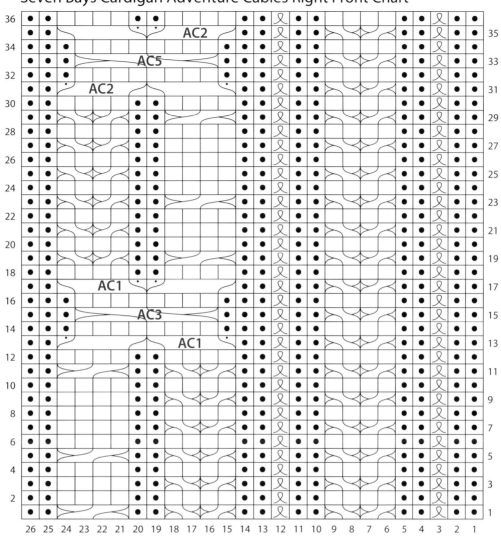

Stitches

- ☐ (RS): Knit, (WS): Purl
- ● (RS): Purl, (WS): Knit
- ⅃ (RS): k-tbl, (WS): p-tbl
- ⟩⟨ 1/1 RT
- ⟩⟨ 1/1 LC
- ▱ 2/2 RC
- ▱ 2/2 LC

Adventure Cables (AC) Stitches

Stitches are noted in pattern after being crossed.

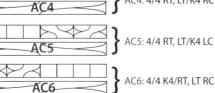

AC1: 4/1 P1/RT, LT LC

AC2: 4/1 RT, LT/P1 RC

AC3: 4/4 K4/RT, LT LC

AC4: 4/4 RT, LT/K4 RC

AC5: 4/4 RT, LT/K4 LC

AC6: 4/4 K4/RT, LT RC

CHART TIPS

Worked flat (read from right to left for RS rows, left to right for WS rows).

Uses cables worked with knit sts.

Uses Adventure Cables (AC) worked with cable sts.

Chart rows are repeatable for pattern length adjustment.

Cont in patt as est, working the 1st st on the RS row as garter, progressing through Adventure Cables Left Front Chart, continuing 3 sts in double knitting (a technique that produces 2 layers of fabric), and working all other sts as stockinette for 20 more rows, ending with a WS row.

Dec Row (RS): K1, k2tog, work in patt to end—1 st decreased.

Rep Dec Row every 20 rows 4 more times—57 (61, 65, 69, 73) (77, 85, 89, 93, 97) sts.

Cont in patt as est, working the 1st st on the RS row as garter, progressing through Adventure Cables Left Front Chart, continuing 3 sts in double knitting, and working all other sts as stockinette until piece measures 18 in./45.5 cm. Place removable marker around the 1st st.

Armholes
Front Decreases
Dec Row (RS): Knit to 3 sts before m, ssk, k1, sm work to end in patt—1 st decreased.

Sizes 60¼ (63¼, 66¼, 71) in./153 (161, 168, 180) cm only: Rep Dec Row every 20 rows 2 (2, 3, 1) more time(s)—56 (60, 64, 68, 72) (76, 82, 86, 89, 95) sts.

Cont in patt as est, working the first st on the RS row as garter, progressing through Adventure Cables Left Front Chart, continuing 3 sts in double knitting, and working all other sts as stockinette until piece measures 6¾ (7, 7½, 8¼, 9¼) (10, 10¾, 11, 11¼, 11½) in./17 (18, 19, 21, 23.5) (25.5, 27.5, 28, 28.5, 29) cm, ending with a WS row.

Shoulder Shaping and Collar
Next Row (RS): BO 26 (30, 34, 38, 42) (46, 52, 56, 59, 65) sts, remove marker, work to end in patt—30 sts rem.

Cont in patt as est, working the first st on the RS row as garter, progressing through Adventure Cables Left Front Chart, and continuing 3 sts in double knitting until piece measures 4¼ (4¼, 4¼, 4½, 4½) (4½, 4¾, 4¾, 5, 5) in./ 11 (11, 11, 11.5, 11.5) (11.5, 12, 12, 12.5, 12.5) cm, ending with a RS row.

BO all sts, cut yarn leaving a 10 in./25.5 cm tail for seaming.

Right Front
Note: If alternating yarn skeins, switch at the beginning of the WS rows for this side.

Using smaller needles, CO 62 (66, 70, 74, 78) (82, 90, 94, 98, 102) sts.

Setup Row (RS): K1, sl1 wyif, k1, p2, k1tbl, p2, k4, p2, k1tbl, p2, [k4, p2] twice, pm, [k2, p2] 8 (9, 10, 11, 12) (13, 15, 16, 17, 18) times, k1.

Next Row (WS): K1, *k2, p2; rep from * to m, sm, [k2, p4] twice, k2, p1tbl, k2, p4, k2, p1tbl, k2, sl1 wyif, k1, sl1 wyif.

Cont in patt, slipping markers for 6 more rows.

Change to larger 32 in./81 cm circular needles.

Pattern Setup Row (RS): K1, sl1 wyif, k1, work Adventure Cables Right Front Chart to m, sm, knit to end.

Next Row (WS): K1, purl to m, sm, work Adventures Cables Right Front Chart to last 3 sts, sl1 wyif, k1, sl1 wyif.

Cont in patt as est, working the first st on the WS row as garter, progressing through Adventure Cables Right Front Chart, continuing 3 sts in double knitting, and working all other sts as stockinette for 20 more rows, ending with a WS row.

Dec Row (RS): Work to last 3 sts, ssk, k1—1 st decreased.

Rep Dec Row every 20 rows 4 more times— 57 (61, 65, 69, 73) (77, 85, 89, 93, 97) sts.

Cont in patt as est, working the first st on the WS row as garter, progressing through Adventure Cables Right Front Chart,

continuing 3 sts in double knitting, and working all other sts as stockinette until piece measures 18 in./45 cm. Place removable marker around the 1st st.

Armholes
Front Decreases
Dec Row (RS): Work to m, sm, k1, k2tog—1 st decreased.

Sizes 60¼ (63¼, 66¼, 71) in./153 (161, 168, 180) cm only: Rep Dec Row every 20 rows 2 (2, 3, 1) more time(s)—56 (60, 64, 68, 72) (76, 82, 86, 89, 95) sts.

Cont in patt as est, working the 1st st on the WS row as garter, progressing through Adventure Cables Right Front Chart, continuing 3 sts in double knitting, and working all other sts as stockinette until piece measures 6¾ (7, 7½, 8¼, 9 ¼) (10, 10¾, 11, 11¼, 11 ½) in./17 (18, 19, 21, 23.5) (25.5, 27.5, 28, 28.5, 29) cm ending with a RS row.

Shoulder Shaping and Collar
Next Row (RS): BO 26 (30, 34, 38, 42) (46, 52, 56, 59, 65) sts, remove marker, work to end in patt—30 sts rem.

Cont in patt as est, working the 1st st on the WS row as garter, progressing through Adventure Cables Right Front Chart, and continuing 3 sts in double knitting until piece measures 4¼ (4¼, 4¼, 4½, 4½) (4½, 4¾, 4¾, 5, 5) in./11 (11, 11, 11.5, 11.5) (11.5, 12, 12, 12.5, 12.5) cm, ending with a WS row.

BO all sts, cut yarn leaving a 10 in./25.5 cm tail for seaming.

Sleeves
Using larger dpns or 16 in./41 cm circular needle, pick up and knit 70 (74, 78, 86, 96) (106, 112, 116, 118, 120) sts evenly around armhole; see tip on this technique on page 21. Join to work in the round and pm for beg of rnd.

Knit 20 (12, 8, 8, 4) (4, 16, 16, 8, 0) rnds even.

Dec Rnd: K1, k2tog, knit to last 3 sts, ssk, k1—2 sts decreased.

Rep Dec Rnd every 9 (8, 7, 6, 5) (4, 3, 3, 3, 3) rnds 10 (12, 14, 16, 21) (26, 27, 27, 28, 29) more times—48 (48, 48, 52, 52) (52, 56, 60, 60, 60) sts. If beg with a 16 in./41 cm circ needle, change to dpns when necessary.

Take a minute to try on the sweater at this point to see how the sleeve fits before continuing to add extra length. You may want to skip straight to the cuff.

Work even if necessary until sleeve measures 18 (18, 18, 18, 17½) (17½, 16½, 16¼, 15, 14) in./45.5 (45.5, 45.5, 45.5, 44.5) (44.5, 42, 41.5, 38, 35.5) cm from pickup.

Change to smaller dpns.

Next Rnd: K1, *p2, k2; rep from * to last 3 sts, p2, k1.

Rep last rnd for 1½ in./4 cm, BO all sts loosely in patt.

Finishing
Using tapestry needle, seam fronts to back from hem up sides and at shoulders. Seam bound-off edges of collar together, and then seam collar to opening on back. Work in any loose ends, and steam block lightly to set patt.

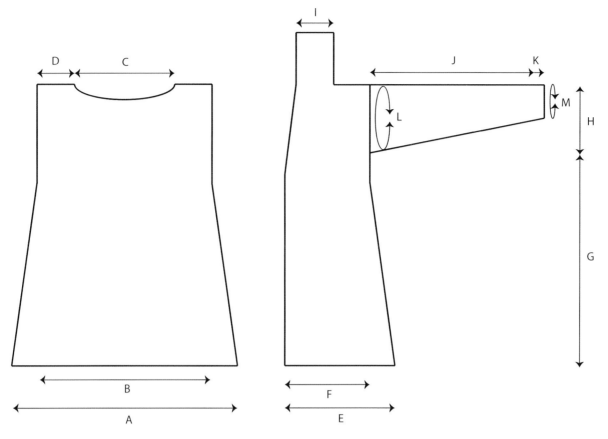

A: 20.5 (22.25, 23.75, 26.75, 28.25)(30, 33, 34.5, 36.25, 39.25) in.
   52 (56.5, 60.5, 68, 72)(76, 84, 87.5, 92, 99.5) cm
B: 18.5 (20.25, 21.75, 24.75, 26.5)(28, 31, 32.75, 34.25, 37.25) in.
   47 (51.5, 55, 63, 67.5)(71, 78.5, 83, 87, 94.5) cm
C: 4.25 (4.25, 4.25, 4.5, 4.5)(4.5, 4.75, 4.75, 5, 5) in.
   11 (11, 11, 11.5, 11.5)(11.5, 12, 12, 12.5, 12.5) cm
D: 5 (5.75, 6.75, 7.5, 8.25)(9, 10.25, 11, 11.5, 12.75) in.
   12.5 (14.5, 17, 19, 21)(23, 26, 28, 29, 32.5) cm
E: 15.5 (16.5, 17.25, 18, 18.75)(19.5, 21, 21.75, 22.5, 23.5) in.
   39.5 (42, 44, 45.5, 47.5)(49.5, 53.5, 55, 57, 59.5) cm
F: 14.5 (15.5, 16.25, 17, 17.75)(18.5, 20, 20.75, 21.75, 22.5) in.
   37 (39.5, 41.5, 43, 45)(47, 51, 52.5, 55, 57) cm
G: 18 in./45.5 cm
H: 6.75 (7, 7.5, 8.25, 9.25) (10, 10.75, 11, 11.25, 11.5) in.
   17 (18, 19, 21, 23.5)(25.5, 27.5, 28, 28.5, 29) cm
I: 3.5 in./9 cm
J: 18 (18, 18, 18, 17.5) (17.5, 16.5, 16.25, 15, 14) in.
   45.5 (45.5, 45.5, 45.5, 44.5)(44.5, 42, 41.5, 38, 35.5) cm
K: 1.5 in./4 cm
L: 13.75 (14.5, 15.25, 16.75, 18.75)(20.75, 21.75, 22.75, 23, 23.5) in.
   35 (37, 38.5, 42.5, 47.5)(52.5, 55, 58, 58.5, 59.5) cm
M: 9.25 (9.25, 9.25, 10.25, 10.25)(10.25, 11, 11.75, 11.75, 11.75) in.
   23.5 (23.5, 23.5, 26, 26)(26, 28, 30, 30, 30) cm

CHAPTER

MOSAIC

CROSSINGS

CROSSINGS WITH

MOSAIC STITCHES

Mosaic stitches are worked by a combination of slipping or knitting regular knit stitches to pull contrasting colors into different rows of knitting. The fun of creating these patterns was finding mosaic stitches that would still read as graphic patterns during the crossings and not visually fall apart. For this chapter, the Adventure Cables are nestled within the mosaic stitches, and all Adventure Cabling will include a combination of either knit or slipped stitches on the crossing. The chapter begins with the Mt. Shuksan Cowl and Karamin Hat, which are both great intros to Adventure Cabling with slipped and knit stitches. The final pattern, Enchantment Lake Cardigan, does not slip any stitches during the Adventure Cable but works a 1/1 right twist stitch for columns of twisted stitches that move over the areas of mosaic patterning.

WHAT TO EXPECT

The "Crossings with Mosaic Stitches" chapter includes moving sections of mosaic patterning; two yarns will be used in each project, but only one yarn at a time. One of the patterns includes a 2-stitch twisted cable on the Adventure Cable within the mosaic patterning.

SKILL LEVELS INCLUDED

"Crossings with Mosaic Stitches" includes two Adventure level patterns where the Adventure Cable uses mosaic stitches and one Be Brave level pattern that uses mosaic stitches and cabling during an Adventure Cable.

Mt. Shuksan Cowl

Cushy garter stitch mosaic patterning is combined with offset cables for a cozy cowl with cable patterning that is almost an optical illusion. A narrow hem of ribbing is worked on either end for added texture and a visual border.

I do love a good cowl. They are so easy to tuck under a coat and never come undone like a scarf does. The straightforward shaping of a simple tube was the perfect canvas for this interesting mosaic crossings pattern that is so much easier than it looks. We have done a fair number of drives through the Rocky Mountains, and I am always keen to see the patterns created by the trees and the snow in the upper reaches of those massive crowns. The stitch pattern on this cowl is a nod to those isolated forests, covered with snow for so many months of the year and mostly visited by prying eyes of passengers riding far below them.

Adventure level/Advanced Intermediate: This pattern has moderate patterning on the Adventure Cable such as increases, decreases, or slipped stitches.

Finished Size
23¼ (30) in./59 (76) cm circumference, 9¼ in./23.5 cm tall, after blocking
    Cowl shown measures 23¼ in./58 cm.

Yarn
Sweet Georgia Superwash DK (#2 fine weight; 100% superwash merino; 256 yd./234 m per 4 oz./115 g): 1 skein Hemlock (MC), 1 skein Snowfall (CC)

Needles
US size 5 (3.75 mm): 16 in./41 cm circular needle

US size 6 (4.0 mm): 16 in./41 cm circular needle

Adjust needle size if necessary to obtain the correct gauge.

Notions
Marker (m); cable needle (cn) optional; tapestry needle

Gauge
24 sts and 46 rnds = 4 in./10 cm in Adventure Cables Pattern on larger needle, after blocking

Pattern Notes

This cowl is worked in the round from the bottom up. Only one color is used at a time. Slip all stitches purlwise with yarn in back.

Alteration Information

Note: *Any alterations made may affect yard-age amounts used.*

✳ Pattern repeats can be added or sub-tracted to change the cowl circumference by altering the cast-on number by 20 stitches.

✳ Chart rows can be repeated as many times as desired to alter height of cowl.

✳ End with Row 6 to have a symmetrical pattern.

✳ A snug cowl that hugs the face should be the same circumference as the head or 1 inch less.

✳ A long infinity scarf that can double up into a cowl should be twice the head circumference plus 2–4 inches.

Stitch Guide

Rib Stitch (multiple of 5 sts)
Rnd 1: K2, *p2, k3; rep from* to last 3 sts, p2, k1.

Rep Rnd 1 for patt.

Adventure Cables Stitch Guide
With Cable Needle
AC1: 4/4 K2, SL1, K1/K2, SL1, K1 LC using **cn:** Slip 4 sts to cn and hold in front, k2, sl1, k1, and then k2, sl1, k1 from cn.

Without Cable Needle
AC1: 4/4 K2, SL1, K1/K2, SL1, K1 LC without **cn:** Reach right needle tip behind work and insert into the 5th, 6th, 7th, and 8th sts from left tip, slide first 8 sts off left tip, reinsert left tip into first 4 sts in front of work, slide 4 sts from right tip back to left tip, [k2, sl1, k1] twice. *See Photo Tutorial on page 154.*

INSTRUCTIONS

Edge

Using smaller needles and MC, cast on 140 (180) sts, join to work in the round, and place marker (m) for beg of rnd.

Work Rib Stitch (see Stitch Guide) until piece measures 1 in./2.5 cm from cast-on edge.

Change to larger needle, attach CC, do not cut MC.

Next Rnd: Knit with CC.

Next Rnd: Purl with CC.

Adventure Cables

Pattern Rnd: Work the charted Adventure Cables Pattern 7 (9) times around.

To do this, cont in patt as est for 77 more rnds, progressing through Rnds 2–24 of Adventure Cables Chart, repeating Rnds 1–24 twice more and working Rnds 1–6 once.

Next Rnd: Knit with CC.

Next Rnd: Purl with CC.

Next Rnd: Knit with MC, cut CC.

Edge
Change to smaller needles, using MC only work Rib Stitch until piece measures 9¼ in./23.5 cm from cast-on edge. BO all sts loosely.

Finishing
Cut yarn, work in any loose ends.

Mt. Shuksan Cowl Adventure Cables Chart

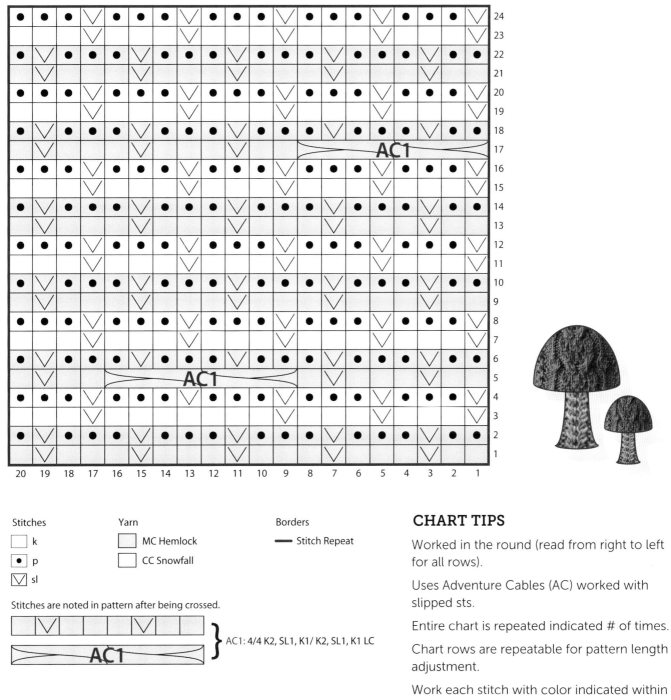

Stitches
- ☐ k
- ● p
- ☑ sl

Yarn
- ☐ MC Hemlock
- ☐ CC Snowfall

Borders
- — Stitch Repeat

Stitches are noted in pattern after being crossed.

} AC1: 4/4 K2, SL1, K1/ K2, SL1, K1 LC

CHART TIPS

Worked in the round (read from right to left for all rows).

Uses Adventure Cables (AC) worked with slipped sts.

Entire chart is repeated indicated # of times.

Chart rows are repeatable for pattern length adjustment.

Work each stitch with color indicated within square.

TUTORIAL: How to Work the Mosaic Adventure Cables without a Cable Needle

The Mt. Shuksan Cowl uses Adventure Cables that continue the mosaic stitch patterning at the same time as the stitch crossings. To do this, the crossed Adventure Cable stitches are worked across with a combination of slipped and knit stitches. Counting the rows between each cable crossing row can be easily achieved by noting the number of color stripes.

On the chart, the Adventure Cable for the Mt. Shuksan Cowl is worked over 8 stitches on rounds 5 and 17. These rnds are worked by knitting stitches with the main color and slipping stitches worked in the contrast color. The definition of AC1 for this pattern is [k2, sl1 wyib, k1] twice.

1. On Rnd 5, work through stitch 8, ready to work stitch 9. The upcoming 8 sts that are going to be used for the Adventure Cable will be 1 MC followed by 3 CC, and again 1 MC followed by 3 CC. The first set of 4 sts will move in front of the second set of 4 sts to create the 4 over 4 left cross cable.

2. Reach the right needle tip behind the work and insert into the 5th, 6th, 7th, and 8th sts from left tip.

3. Slip all 8 sts off the left tip.

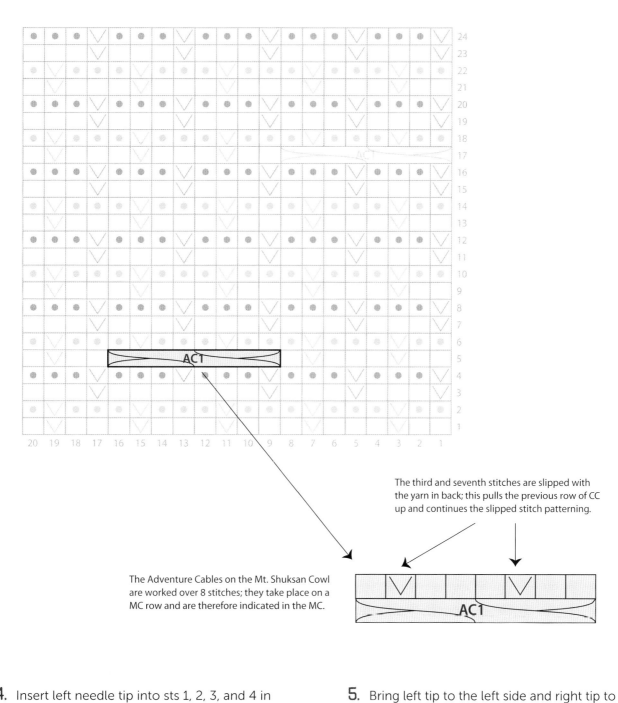

The third and seventh stitches are slipped with the yarn in back; this pulls the previous row of CC up and continues the slipped stitch patterning.

The Adventure Cables on the Mt. Shuksan Cowl are worked over 8 stitches; they take place on a MC row and are therefore indicated in the MC.

4. Insert left needle tip into sts 1, 2, 3, and 4 in front of work.

5. Bring left tip to the left side and right tip to the right side.

6. Slip 4 sts from right tip back to left tip.

7. All sts are on left tip.

8. Knit 2 with MC.

9. And slip the next stitch with yarn in back.

10. Finish out the patterning of MC k3, CC sl1, MC k1.

Tip: I am a very visual knitter who hates counting rows/rnds. I found it especially helpful to place a removable marker into the work after completing Rnd 5 to indicate that this MC rnd was the Adventure Cable Rnd. It was very easy at that point to count the 2 even MC stripes worked in between the Adventure Cable rnds and know that the following MC stripe was Rnd 17 (the 2nd Adventure Cable rnd). You can apply this idea to any of the mosaic charts by placing a removable marker on the Adventure Cables row and then counting the number of stripes to the next Adventure Cables row.

Karamin Hat

Vertical track mosaic stitch patterns are crossed over one another in this clever and graphic hat. One color is used at a time with cushy garter stitch worked in between the vertical Adventure Cables for a cozy head topper.

This mosaic stitch pattern has always been one of my favorites and was the first mosaic pattern I tried adding cables into. I wanted the vibe of a traditional basic cabled hat that would showcase really clearly the technique of crossed mosaic stitches. The golden yellow and worn beige colors were inspired by early morning light, faded wooden porches, waving fields of grass, and leaning weathered fence posts.

Adventure level/Advanced Intermediate:
This pattern has moderate patterning on the Adventure Cable such as increases, decreases, or slipped stitches.

Finished Size
18 (19½, 21, 22½) in./45.5 (49.5, 53.5, 57) cm head circumference
Hat shown measures 21 in./53.5 cm, modeled with 1 in./2.5 cm of negative ease.

Yarn
Berroco Ultra Wool DK (#3 light weight; 100% superwash wool; 292 yd./267 m per 3.5 oz./100 g): 1 ball #83104 Driftwood (MC), 1 ball #8329 Butternut (CC)

Needles

US size 5 (3.75 mm): 16 in./41 cm circular needle

US size 6 (4.0 mm): 16 in./41 cm circular needle and set of double-pointed needles (dpns)

Adjust needle size if necessary to obtain the correct gauge.

Notions
Marker (m), cable needle (cn) optional, tapestry needle

Gauge
24 sts and 44 rnds = 4 in./10 cm in Adventure Cables Pattern on larger needle

Pattern Notes

This hat is worked in the round from the bottom up. Only one color is used at a time. Slip all stitches purlwise with yarn in back.

Stitch Guide

Rib Stitch (multiple of 3 sts)
Rnd 1: *K2, p1; rep from* to m.

Rep Rnd 1 for patt.

Adventure Cables Stitch Guide
With Cable Needle
AC1: 3/3 K3/SL1, K1, SL1 LC using cn: Slip 3 sts to cn and hold in front, k3, sl1, k1, sl1 from cn.

AC2: 3/3 SL1, K1, SL1/K3 LC using cn: Slip 3 sts to cn and hold in front, sl1, k1, sl1, k3 from cn.

Without Cable Needle
AC1: 3/3 K3/SL1, K1, SL1 LC without cn: Reach right needle tip behind work and insert into the 4th, 5th, and 6th sts from left tip, slide first 6 sts off left tip, reinsert left tip into first 3 sts in front of work, slide 3 sts from right tip back to left tip, k3, sl1, k1, sl1.

AC2: 3/3 SL1, K1, SL1/K3 LC without cn: Reach right needle tip behind work and insert into the 4th, 5th, and 6th sts from left tip, slide first 6 sts off left tip, reinsert left tip into first 3 sts in front of work, slide 3 sts from right tip back to left tip, sl1, k1, sl1, k3.

INSTRUCTIONS

Brim

Using smaller needles and MC, cast on 108 (117, 126, 135) sts using the Old Norwegian method (*see Tutorial on page 39*) or equally stretchy method of your choice. Place marker (pm), and join in the rnd.

Work Rib Stitch (see Stitch Guide) until piece measures 1¾ in./4.5 cm from cast-on edge.

Change to larger needle, attach CC, do not cut MC.

Next Rnd: Knit with CC.

Next Rnd: Purl with CC.

Adventure Cables

Pattern Rnd: Work the charted Adventure Cables Pattern 12 (13, 14, 15) times around.

Cont in patt as est, progressing through Adventure Cables Pattern until piece measures 6 (6¼, 6½, 6¾) in./13.5 (16, 16.5, 17) cm from cast-on edge, ending with Rnd 4, 8, 14, 18, 22, or 24.

Decreases

If last rnd worked was 4, 8, or 24, use Decrease Pattern 1; if last rnd worked was 14, 18, or 22, use Decrease Pattern 2.

Next Rnd: Work the charted Decrease Pattern 1 or 2; 12 (13, 14, 15) times around—12 (13, 14, 15) sts dec'd.

Cont in patt as established, progressing through 20 rows of Decrease Pattern; if Decrease Pattern 1 was used, cut CC and use MC only; if Decrease Pattern 2 was used, cut MC and use CC only.

Next Rnd: Knit.

Dec Rnd: *K2tog; rep from * around—12 (13, 14, 15) sts.

Finishing

Cut yarn. Using tapestry needle, thread end through rem sts, pull tight, and fasten off. Work in any loose ends, and block lightly if desired.

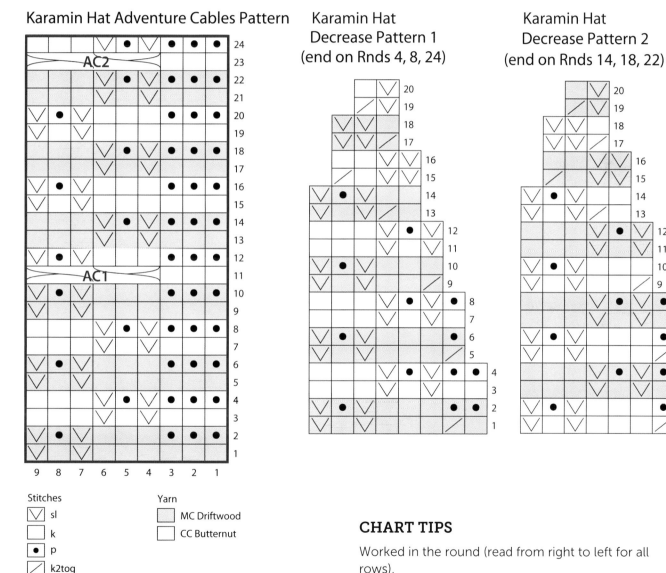

Karamin Hat Adventure Cables Pattern

Karamin Hat
Decrease Pattern 1
(end on Rnds 4, 8, 24)

Karamin Hat
Decrease Pattern 2
(end on Rnds 14, 18, 22)

Stitches

- ⟨V⟩ sl
- ☐ k
- • p
- ⟋ k2tog

Yarn

- ▢ MC Driftwood
- ☐ CC Butternut

Adventure Cables (AC) Stitches
Stitches are noted in pattern after being crossed.

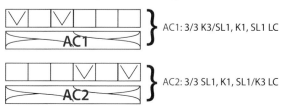

AC1: 3/3 K3/SL1, K1, SL1 LC

AC2: 3/3 SL1, K1, SL1/K3 LC

CHART TIPS

Worked in the round (read from right to left for all rows).

Uses Adventure Cables (AC) worked with slipped sts.

Entire chart is repeated indicated # of times.

Chart rows are repeatable for pattern length adjustment.

Work each stitch with color indicated within square.

Enchantment Lake Cardigan

This colorful cardigan has a wide swath of cabled mosaic stitches that is worked all in one piece from the front hem, around the upper back, and down again. The back is worked separately in the single main color using stockinette stitch, so this cardigan requires some seaming along the side and upper back. The twisted stitch cables in the main color are worked at the same time as the crossed stitches, giving this pattern a Be Brave level.

For this cardigan, I really wanted to have the pattern band run up the front of each side and around the back without a seam at the back neck. The cabled mosaic patterning was so beautiful and reminiscent of waves that I just couldn't bear to work it in two pieces with a seam at the back neck. As a result, this cardigan does have some seaming on the sides and upper back that connect the stockinette back to the fronts. The stitch pattern and colors are inspired by sunset on a beautiful lake, listening to the waves lap at the pier as the light seeps away from the world for the day.

Be Brave level/Experienced: This pattern has intricate patterning on the Adventure Cable such as crossed stitches or stranded colorwork stitches.

Finished Sizes

34 (38, 42, 46, 50) (54, 58, 62, 66, 70) in./86.5 (96.5, 106.5, 117, 127) (137, 147.5, 157.5, 167.5, 178) cm bust circumference
Shown in size 42, modeled with 3 in./7.5 cm of positive ease.

Yarn

Berroco Yarn Ultra Wool Worsted (#4 medium weight; 100% superwash wool; 219 yd./200 m per 3.5 oz./100 g): 4 (5, 5, 6, 6) (7, 8, 8, 9, 9) balls #3364 Lake (MC)

Berroco Yarn Sesame (#4 medium weight; 43% wool, 39% acrylic, 9% cotton, 9% nylon; 230 yd./210 m per 3.5 oz./100 g): 2 (2, 2, 2, 2) (2, 3, 3, 3, 3) balls #7448 Zen Garden (CC)

Needles

US sizes 6 (4.0 mm) and 7 (4.5 mm): 32 in./81 cm circular or straight needles, and double-pointed needles (dpns). Adjust needle size if necessary to obtain the correct gauge.

Notions

1 stitch marker (m), 8 removable stitch markers, cable needle (cn) optional, tapestry needle

Gauge

18 sts and 25 rows = 4 in./10 cm in stockinette stitch

27¾ sts and 36 rows = 4 in./10 cm over Adventure Cables Pattern, lightly steam blocked

16 sts and 36 rows = 4 in./10 cm over garter stitch

Pattern Notes

The Adventure Cables Panel is worked all in one piece. Removable markers are placed to indicate armhole depth and seaming placements. The Mosaic Chart uses the MC and CC alternating every 2 rows; work each entire row with the color indicated by the chart, even the preceding garter stitches.

An important note on sleeves: The sleeves are picked up and worked from the top down in the round, but they sit lower on the upper arm than a typical sleeve. To check your upper arm size, start with the width of the front band for your size and multiply this width by 0.75. Then, starting at your center back neck, measure down over your shoulder the resulting measurement. This is where the top of your sleeve will sit, and this is where you should measure the upper sleeve circumference. This is also a great time to see whether the sleeve length will fit you; measure from this spot to the cuff you desire and compare to the schematic for your size.

Alteration information

Note: *Any alterations made may affect yardage amounts used.*

* If you need to add width to the front band, you can increase the number of garter stitches worked between the beginning of the right-side row and the Adventure Cables Pattern.
* If you are adding back width to your size, you will need to add the same amount to the length worked between the two top armhole markers on the front band of Adventure Cables.
* Any added armhole depth should be inserted between the first and second and the third and fourth removable markers when working the front band.

Add the same amount of depth to the back between the armhole depth marker and the first set of bound-off stitches.

* If altering the armhole depth to adjust the upper-arm circumference, please see page 19.

Stitch Guide

1/1RT: Insert right tip into 2 sts as if to k2tog, wrap and pull through, do not drop off left needle; insert right tip into back of 1st st on left tip, wrap and pull through, drop all sts off left needle.

Adventure Cables Stitch Guide
With Cable Needle
AC1: 6/6 K4, RT/K4, RT RC with cn: Slip 6 sts to cn and hold in back, k4, RT, and then k4, RT from cn.

AC2: 6/6 RT, K4/RT, K4 LC with cn: Slip 6 sts to cn and hold in front, RT, k4, and then RT, k4 from cn.

Without Cable Needle
AC1: 6/6 K4, RT/K4, RT RC without cn: Reach right needle tip in front of work and insert into the 7th, 8th, 9th, 10th, 11th, and 12th sts from left tip, slide all 12 sts off left tip, reinsert left tip into first 6 sts behind work, slide 6 sts from right tip back to left tip, [k4, RT] twice.

AC2: 6/6 RT, K4/RT, K4 LC without cn: Reach right needle tip behind work and insert into the 7th, 8th, 9th, 10th, 11th, and 12th sts from left tip, slide all 12 sts off left tip, reinsert left tip into first 6 sts in front of work, slide 6 sts from right tip back to left tip, [RT, k4] twice.

INSTRUCTIONS

Back
Using smaller needles and MC, CO 77 (86, 95, 104, 113) (122, 131, 140, 149, 158) sts.

Knit 10 rows. Change to larger needles.

Next Row (RS): Knit to end.

Next Row (WS): K1, purl to last st, k1.

Cont in patt as est, working first and last sts as garter and all other sts as stockinette until piece measures 13 in./33 cm from cast-on edge.

Place removable markers into each side of work; these are the armhole bottom markers.

Cont in patt as est, working first and last sts as garter and all other sts as stockinette until piece measures 5¾ (6, 6½, 7¼, 8¼) (9, 9¾, 10, 10¼, 10¼) in./14.5 (15, 16.5, 18.5, 21) (23, 25, 25.5, 26, 26) cm from marked row. If altering the upper-arm circumference, this is the measurement to adjust.

Enchantment Lake Cardigan Adventure Cables Chart

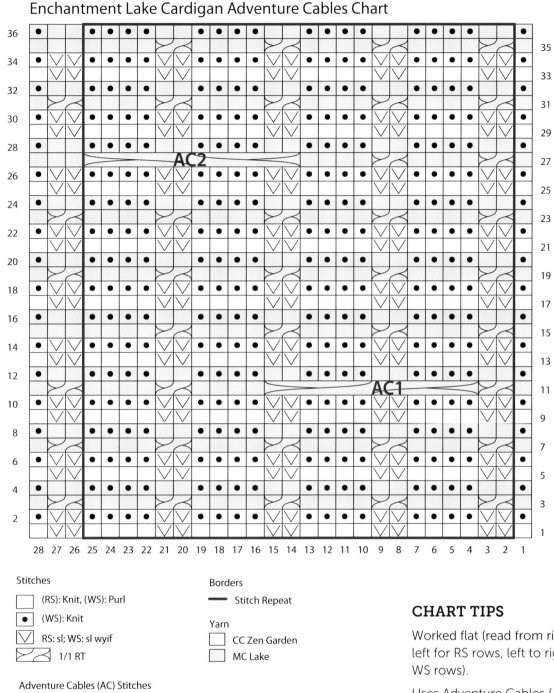

Stitches

☐ (RS): Knit, (WS): Purl

• (WS): Knit

∨ RS: sl; WS: sl wyif

⧄ 1/1 RT

Borders

— Stitch Repeat

Yarn

☐ CC Zen Garden

☐ MC Lake

Adventure Cables (AC) Stitches

Stitches are noted in pattern after being crossed.

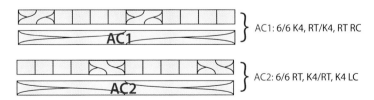

AC1: 6/6 K4, RT/K4, RT RC

AC2: 6/6 RT, K4/RT, K4 LC

CHART TIPS

Worked flat (read from right to left for RS rows, left to right for WS rows).

Uses Adventure Cables (AC) worked with cabled sts.

Has a stitch repeat; repeat stitches enclosed in red box indicated # of times.

Chart rows are repeatable for pattern length adjustment.

Work each stitch with color indicated within square.

BO 6 (7, 8, 10, 11) (12, 14, 15, 16, 18) sts at beg of next 6 rows—41 (44, 47, 44, 47) (50, 47, 50, 53, 50) sts rem. BO all sts.

Fronts (worked as one piece)

Using smaller needles and MC, CO 57 (61, 65, 80, 84) (88, 92, 106, 110, 114) sts.

Knit 3 rows.

Setup Row (WS): K52 (52, 52, 76, 76) (76, 76, 100, 100, 100), pm, knit to end.

Join CC and change to larger needles.

Pattern Row (RS): Knit to m, sm, work Adventure Cables Chart to end.

Next Row (WS): Work Adventure Cables Chart to m, sm, knit to end.

Cont in patt as est, working sts between the beg of the RS row and marker as garter stitch and sts between marker and end of RS row in Adventure Cables Chart, until piece measures 13 in./33 cm from cast-on edge, place removable marker into beg of work for Left Side armhole bottom.

Cont in patt as est until piece measures 5¾ (6, 6½, 7¼, 8¼) (9, 9¾, 10, 10¼, 10¼) in./14.5 (15, 16.5, 18.5, 21) (23, 25, 25.5, 26, 26) cm from last marked row, place removable marker into beg of work for Left Side armhole top. If altering the upper-arm circumference, this is the measurement to adjust.

Cont in patt as est until piece measures 17 (19, 21, 23, 25) (27, 29, 31, 33, 35) in./43 (48.5, 53.5, 58.5, 63.5) (68.5, 73.5, 78.5, 84, 89) cm from last marked row, place removable marker into beg of work for Right Side arm-hole top. If altering the circumference, add

length to this measurement to match the added back width.

Cont in patt as est until piece measures 5¾ (6, 6½, 7¼, 8¼) (9, 9¾, 10, 10¼, 10¼) in./14.5 (15, 16.5, 18.5, 21) (23, 25, 25.5, 26, 26) cm from last marked row, place removable marker into beg of work for Right Side armhole bottom. If altering the upper-arm circumference, this is the measurement to adjust.

Cont in patt as est until piece measures 12¾ in./32.5 cm from last marked row. Change to smaller needles, cut CC, using MC only knit 3 rows. BO all sts on WS knitwise.

Seaming

Using tapestry needle and 15 in./38 cm length of yarn, seam Front Band to Back between cast-on and Left Side armhole bottom marker, work in yarn end. Using tapestry needle and 21 (23, 25, 27, 29) (31, 33, 35, 37, 39) in./53.5 (58.5, 63.5, 68.5, 73.5) (78.5, 84, 89, 94, 99) cm length of yarn, seam Front Band between Left Side armhole top marker, and Right Side armhole top marker to Back bound-off edge and work in yarn end. Using tapestry needle and 15 in./38 cm length of yarn, seam Front Band to Back between Right Side armhole bottom marker and bound-off edge, work in end of yarn.

Sleeves

Using larger dpns, MC, and beginning at bottom of armhole, pick up and knit 52 (54, 58, 64, 74) (80, 88, 90, 92, 92) sts around, join to work in rnd and place marker to indicate beg of rnd.

Knit 0 (6, 8, 12, 3) (9, 15, 9, 6, 3) rnds even.

Dec Rnd: K1, k2tog, knit to last 3 sts, ssk, k1.

Rep Dec Rnd every 12 (10, 8, 6, 5) (4, 3, 3, 3, 3) rnds 7 (8, 10, 13, 17) (20, 23, 23, 23, 22) more times—36 (36, 36, 36, 38) (38, 40, 42, 44, 46) sts.

Work even if necessary until sleeve measures 16 (16, 16, 16, 15½) (15½, 14½, 13½, 13, 12) in./40.5 (40.5, 40.5, 40.5, 39.5) (39.5, 37, 34.5, 33, 30.5) cm from pickup rnd.

Change to smaller needles.

Next Rnd: Purl around.

Next Rnd: Knit around.

Rep last 2 rnds once more.

Next Rnd: Purl around. BO all sts knitwise.

Finishing
Work in any loose ends and steam block lightly to set patt.

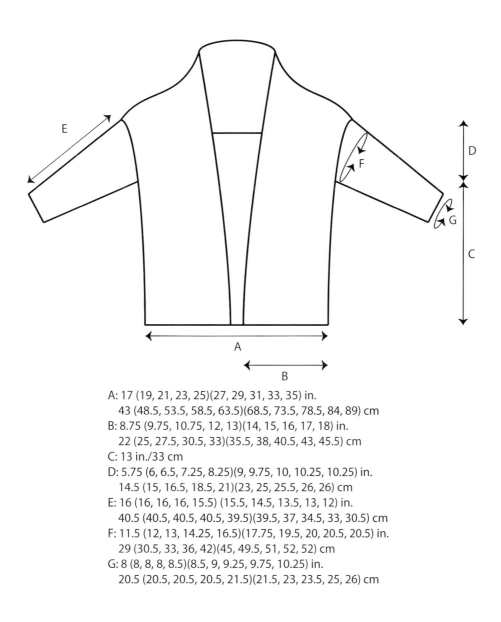

A: 17 (19, 21, 23, 25)(27, 29, 31, 33, 35) in.
   43 (48.5, 53.5, 58.5, 63.5)(68.5, 73.5, 78.5, 84, 89) cm
B: 8.75 (9.75, 10.75, 12, 13)(14, 15, 16, 17, 18) in.
   22 (25, 27.5, 30.5, 33)(35.5, 38, 40.5, 43, 45.5) cm
C: 13 in./33 cm
D: 5.75 (6, 6.5, 7.25, 8.25)(9, 9.75, 10, 10.25, 10.25) in.
   14.5 (15, 16.5, 18.5, 21)(23, 25, 25.5, 26, 26) cm
E: 16 (16, 16, 16, 15.5) (15.5, 14.5, 13.5, 13, 12) in.
   40.5 (40.5, 40.5, 40.5, 39.5)(39.5, 37, 34.5, 33, 30.5) cm
F: 11.5 (12, 13, 14.25, 16.5)(17.75, 19.5, 20, 20.5, 20.5) in.
   29 (30.5, 33, 36, 42)(45, 49.5, 51, 52, 52) cm
G: 8 (8, 8, 8, 8.5)(8.5, 9, 9.25, 9.75, 10.25) in.
   20.5 (20.5, 20.5, 20.5, 21.5)(21.5, 23, 23.5, 25, 26) cm

CHAPTER

STRANDED

CROSSINGS

CROSSINGS WITH

STRANDED STITCHES

Stranded colorwork is some of the most magical knitting. Using only stockinette stitches and different colors, amazing graphic motifs can be added into any garment or accessory. Because the stitches are all worked in stockinette, the Adventure Cables worked with Stranded Knitting involve changing colors while working the stitches in a different order or carrying the unused colors behind the crossed stitches. Two of the patterns in this chapter have color changes during the Adventure Cables, while one has cables worked in a single color within a background of stranded patterning. All three of the patterns are worked in the round, on either circular needles or double-pointed needles.

WHAT TO EXPECT

The "Crossings with Stranded Stitches" chapter includes both moving sections of single color stockinette inside stranded patterning and moving sections of stranded patterning inside itself. All charts are worked in the round, and floats should be kept loose on the back of the work.

SKILL LEVELS INCLUDED

"Crossings with Stranded Stitches" includes one Explore level pattern and two Be Brave level patterns.

Birdsview Scarf

Worked in the round, this extra cushy and thick scarf has regular knit cables nestled within the stranded patterning. Even though this pattern has both stranded patterning and cables, they are not worked at the same time. Carry the floats loosely behind the cabled stitches. Slipped stitches are worked every second round to create a fold in the fabric and help it lie flat. The edges are worked with a 2x2 ribbing pattern. The scarf is intentionally shorter to loop around the back neck once, but this pattern is easily repeatable for any length of scarf desired.

This scarf was designed with my husband in mind—he loves to have a warm and squishy scarf to keep the chill away but hates to have that scarf in front of his neck. This scarf is worked double thick in the round, is wide enough to cover the back of his neck from under the collar to hairline, and long enough to just cross over in front, creating a V-neck shape. The colors were chosen from a long-ago and barely remembered camp T-shirt with excellent 1970s harvest gold and russet orange on a mild beige background.

Explore level/Intermediate: This pattern has very simple patterning on the Adventure Cable such as knits and purls.

Finished Size
9 in./23 cm wide and 40 ¾ in./103.5 cm long

Yarn
Plymouth Yarn Company Worsted Merino Superwash (#4 medium weight; 100% superwash merino wool; 218 yd./199 m per 4 oz./100 g): 3 skeins #65 Fox (MC), 1 skein #61 Gold (CC1), 1 skein #40 Pumpkin (CC2)

Needles
US size 7 (4.5 mm): 16 in./41 cm circular or double-pointed needles (dpns). Adjust needle size if necessary to obtain the correct gauge.

Notions
Cable needle (cn) optional, tapestry needle

Gauge
24 ¾ sts and 24 rnds = 4 in./10 cm over charted patt, after blocking

Pattern Notes

This scarf is worked in the round; it is essentially a tube, so all rounds are worked and seen from the right side of the work. The scarf is divided into the front and back with the first and last stitches of the front and back slipped knitwise with the yarn in back every 2 rounds. This creates a fold in the scarf and helps it lie flat. Carry any floats along the back of the work very loosely; since the cabled stitches pull in, it is very important to spread them out after cabling and before stringing along the float behind the work. On Rnds 1 and 3, *do not* tuck floats between stitches 9 and 10—if tucked in this area, they will be visible when the cables are worked on Rnd 4. Instead, tuck floats between stitches 8 and 9 or 10 and 11.

Alteration Information

Note: *Any alterations made may affect yardage amounts used.*

- ✳ Additional repeats of the chart can be worked to increase the length of this scarf. For a mirror-image scarf, repeat Rnds 1–20 as many times as desired, and then work Rnds 1–10 once.
- ✳ Width can be increased by adding multiples of 36 sts to the cast-on. For each multiple of 36 added, work [k1, p1] an additional 9 times on Rnd 1 of pattern, and work chart 4 times on Pattern Setup Rnd.
- ✳ If a smaller gauge yarn is desired, this pattern would work best as written for a DK weight, or add 36 sts to the cast-on for a sport or fingering weight to get *approximately* the same size scarf. Work as many round repeats as necessary for desired length.

Stitch Guide

2/2 RC with cn: Slip 2 sts to cn and hold in back, k2, k2 from cn.

2/2 LC with cn: Slip 2 sts to cn and hold in front, k2, k2 from cn.

2/2 RC without cn: Reach right tip in front of work and insert into the 3rd and 4th sts from left tip, slide 4 sts off left tip, reinsert left tip into first 2 sts behind work, slide 2 sts from right tip to left tip, k4.

2/2 LC without cn: Reach right tip behind work and insert into the 3rd and 4th sts from left tip, slide 4 sts off left tip, reinsert left tip into first 2 sts in front of work, slide 2 sts from right tip to left tip, k4.

INSTRUCTIONS

CO 112 sts using the Old Norwegian method (*see Tutorial on page 39*) or stretchy method of your choice. Join to work in the rnd and pm to indicate beg of rnd.

Edging

Rnd 1: *Sl1 wyib, [p2, k2] 13 times, p2, sl1 wyib, pm; rep from * once, last pm is beg of rnd m.

Rnd 2: *K1, [p2, k2] 13 times, p2, k1, sm; rep from * once.

Cont in patt as est, repeating Rnds 1–2, until piece measures 1¾ in./4.5 cm from cast-on edge.

Charted Pattern

Pattern Setup Rnd: [Sl1 wyib, work Chart 3 times, sl1 wyib, sm] twice.

Rnd 2: [K1, work Chart 3 times, k1, sm] twice.

Cont in patt as est for 229 more rnds, working Charted pattern Rnds 2–20 once, Rnds 1–20 10 more times, and 1–10 once.

Edging

Rnd 1: *Sl1 wyib, [p2, k2] 13 times, p2, sl1 wyib, sm; rep from * once.

Rnd 2: *K1, [p2, k2] 13 times, p2, k1, sm; rep from * once.

Cont in patt as est, repeating Rnds 1–2, until ribbing measures 1¾ in./4.5 cm from charted work.

BO all sts loosely.

Finishing

Steam block scarf to fix any tension issues, turn scarf inside out, to work in any loose ends.

Birdsview Scarf Chart

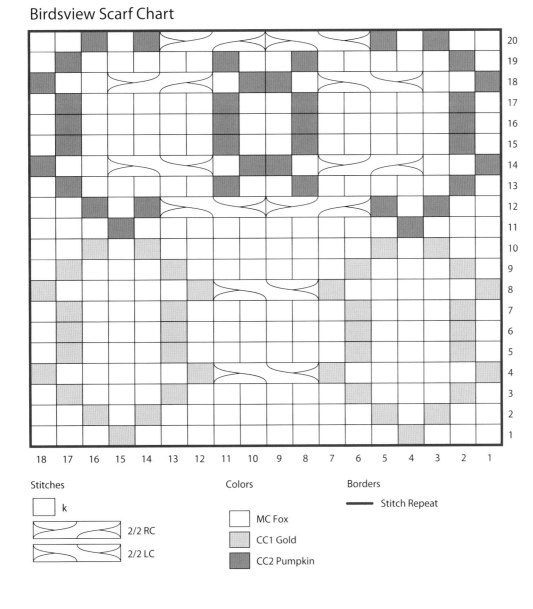

CHART TIPS

Worked in the round (read from right to left for all rows).

Uses cables worked with knit stitches.

Entire chart is repeated indicated # of times.

Work each stitch with color indicated within square.

Stitches

☐ k

⬡ 2/2 RC

⬡ 2/2 LC

Colors

☐ MC Fox

☐ CC1 Gold

⬛ CC2 Pumpkin

Borders

▬ Stitch Repeat

Tekoa Mittens

A fun play on mirror imaging and contrast colors, the Tekoa Mittens use a simple geometric pattern that alternates the main color and contrast color with a cable down the top. Worked in the round from the cuff up, these mittens have a gusseted thumb and narrow ribbed cuff.

I like gusseted mittens the best. I think they fit the hand better than the afterthought thumb method, and so even in colorwork I like to design with a gusset. For this stitch pattern, I was really keen on creating a pattern that could have two sections of the same patterning but in opposite colors. On the palm of the mitten, these two sections sit beside each other as mirror images; on the top of the mitten, one section of the patterning twists over the other, moving the contrasting colors around each other. Red and turquoise are two of my favorite colors and are especially great when they are at a similar vibrancy. They make me think of bright red canoes, skimming across cerulean waters toward tiny square cabins along the shore in the distance.

Be Brave level/Experienced: This pattern has intricate patterning on the Adventure Cable such as crossed stitches or stranded colorwork stitches.

Finished Size
7½ (8½, 9½) in./19 (21.5, 24) cm hand circumference and 9¼ (10¼, 10¾) in./23.5 (26, 27.5) cm total length, including cuff
Mittens shown measure 8½ in./21.5 cm long.

Yarn
Sweet Georgia Yarn Tough Love Sock (#4 medium weight; 80% superwash merino, 20% nylon; 425 yd./388 m per 4 oz./115 g): 1 skein each Cherry (MC) and Mint Julep (CC)

Needles
US size 1 (2.25 mm) set of double-pointed needles (dpns). Adjust needle size if necessary to obtain the correct gauge.

Notions
5 markers, cable needle (cn) optional, stitch holders, tapestry needle

Gauge
37 sts and 41 rnds = 4 in./10 cm over MC Chart and CC Chart, after blocking

10 sts = 1 in./2.5 cm over Adventure Cables Chart, after blocking

Pattern Notes

These mittens are worked from the bottom up in the round. The top of the mitten has more stitches than the bottom of the mitten, so additional decreases are worked only on the top at the beginning of the decrease chart. The beg of the rnd is placed in the center of the mitten palm to prevent a jog in the color change.

Adventure Cables Stitch Guide

With Cable Needle

AC1: 5/5 MC/CC RC using cn: Slip 5 sts to cn and hold in back, [MC k1, CC k1] twice, MC k1, and then [CC k1, MC k1] twice, CC k1, from cn.

AC2: 5/5 CC/MC RC using cn: Slip 5 sts to cn and hold in back, [CC k1, MC k1] twice, CC k1, and then [MC k1, CC k1] twice, MC k1, from cn.

Without Cable Needle

AC1: 5/5 MC/CC RC without cn: Reach right needle tip in front of work and insert into the 6th, 7th, 8th, 9th, and 10th sts from left tip, slide all 10 sts off left tip, reinsert left tip into 1st 5 sts behind work, slide 5 sts from right tip back to left tip, [MC k1, CC k1] twice, MC k1, [CC k1, MC k1] twice, CC k1.

AC2: 5/5 CC/MC RC without cn: Reach right needle tip in front of work and insert into the 6th, 7th, 8th, 9th, and 10th sts from left tip, slide all 10 sts off left tip, reinsert left tip into first 5 sts behind work, slide 5 sts from right tip back to left tip, [CC k1, MC k1] twice, CC k1, [MC k1, CC k1] twice, MC k1.

INSTRUCTIONS

Cuff

Using MC, CO 70 (80, 90) sts using the Old Norwegian method (*see Tutorial on page 39*) or an equally stretchy method. Join to work in the rnd and pm to indicate beg of rnd.

Rnd 1: *P1, k3, p1; rep from * around.

Rep Rnd 1 five more times.

Attach CC, knit 1 round in CC only. Do not cut MC.

Pattern Setup Rnd: Work CC Chart 6 (7, 8) times, pm, work Adventure Cables Chart once, pm, work MC Chart 6 (7, 8) times.

Cont in patt, progressing in all charts for 17 more rnds, ending with Rnd 18 of all charts.

Left Hand Gusset Placement Rnd: Work 17 (17, 22) sts in patt as est, pm, work Left Hand Gusset Chart for the size worked, pm, work to end in patt as est—2 sts increased, 3 sts in between gusset markers.

Cont in patt, progressing in all charts for 23 (27, 29) more rnds, completing Rnds 2–24 (28, 30) of Gusset Charts—90 (104, 118) sts total, including 21 (25, 29) gusset sts between gusset markers.

Next Rnd: Work to gusset marker, remove marker, place foll 21 (25, 29) sts onto a holder or waste yarn; CO 1 st using the Backward Loop Method, remove m, work in patt to end—70 (80, 90) sts.

Cont in patt, progressing in all charts for 33 (36, 38) more rnds, ending with Rnd 20 (25, 1) of all charts.

Tekoa Mittens MC Chart

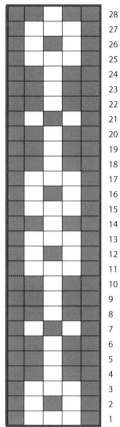

Tekoa Mittens Adventure Cables Chart

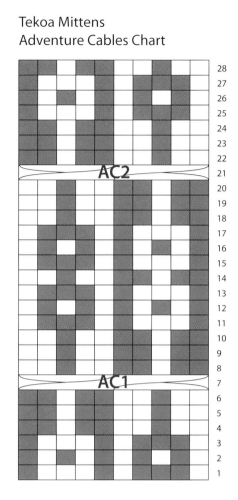

Tekoa Mittens CC Chart

Stitches

▨	k with MC Cherry
☐	k with CC Mint Julep
⧄	M1R with MC
⧄	M1R with CC
⧅	M1L with MC
⧅	M1L with CC
⧄	k2tog with MC
⧄	k2tog with CC
⧅	ssk with MC
⧅	ssk with CC

Borders

—— Stitch Repeat

Adventure Cables (AC) Stitches
Stitches are noted in pattern after being crossed.

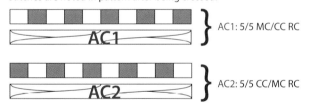

AC1: 5/5 MC/CC RC

AC2: 5/5 CC/MC RC

CHART TIPS

Worked in the round (read from right to left for all rows).

Uses Adventure Cables (AC) worked with stranded sts.

Entire chart is repeated indicated # of times.

Work each stitch with color indicated within square.

Tekoa Mittens Size Small Left Mitten Gusset Chart

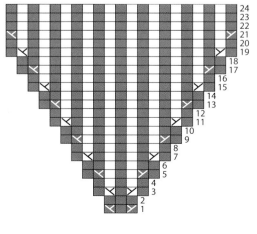

Tekoa Mittens Size Medium Left Mitten Gusset Chart

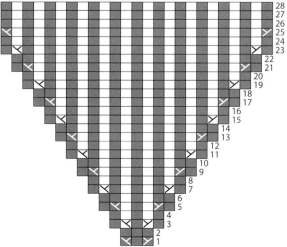

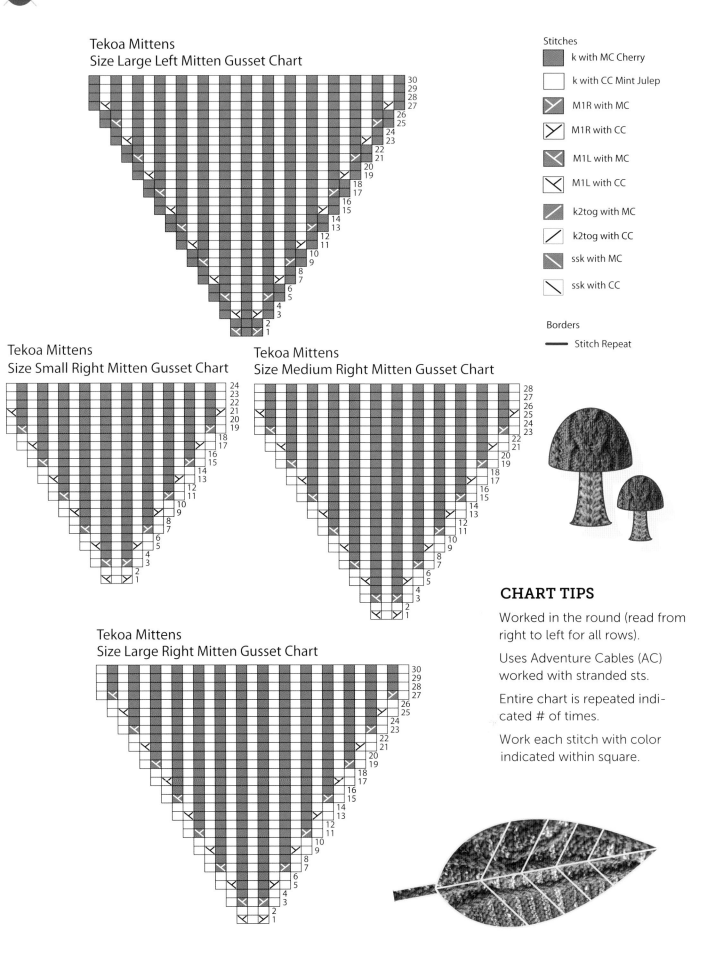

Tekoa Mittens
Size Large Left Mitten Gusset Chart

Tekoa Mittens
Size Small Right Mitten Gusset Chart

Tekoa Mittens
Size Medium Right Mitten Gusset Chart

Tekoa Mittens
Size Large Right Mitten Gusset Chart

Stitches

	k with MC Cherry
	k with CC Mint Julep
	M1R with MC
	M1R with CC
	M1L with MC
	M1L with CC
	k2tog with MC
	k2tog with CC
	ssk with MC
	ssk with CC

Borders

— Stitch Repeat

CHART TIPS

Worked in the round (read from right to left for all rows).

Uses Adventure Cables (AC) worked with stranded sts.

Entire chart is repeated indicated # of times.

Work each stitch with color indicated within square.

Tekoa Mittens Size Small Decrease Chart

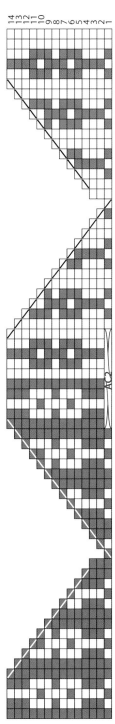

Tekoa Mittens Size Medium Decrease Chart

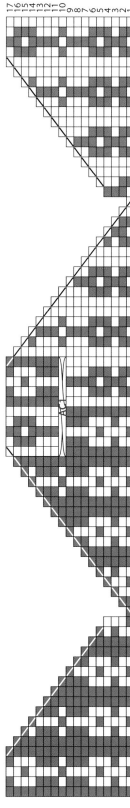

Tekoa Mittens Size Large Decrease Chart

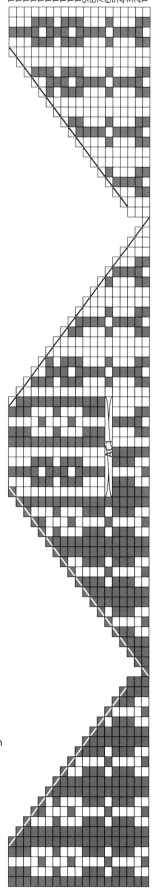

Adventure Cables (AC) Stitches
Stitches are noted in pattern after being crossed.

AC1: 5/5 MC/CC RC

AC2: 5/5 CC/MC RC

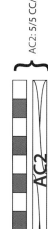

Decreases

Work Decrease Chart for size worked as indicated—20 sts.

Arrange sts so that there are 10 sts on each of 2 needles with the beginning of the rnd in the middle of 1 needle [the palm side], the 4 decreases on either end of each needle, and palm side of work up. Remove beg of rnd marker.

Cut CC leaving a 10 in./25 cm tail, cut MC leaving a 5 in./12.5 cm tail. Using tapestry needle and CC bring yarn to right-hand side of work and close sts using Kitchener Stitch.

Right Mitten

Work same as Left Mitten until Gusset Placement Rnd.

Right Hand Gusset Placement Rnd: Work 52 (62, 67) sts in patt as est, pm, work Right Hand Gusset Chart for the size worked, pm, work to end in patt as est—2 sts increased, 3 sts in between gusset markers.

Work same as Left Mitten to end.

Left Mitten Thumb

Place 21 (25, 29) sts onto dpns, beg at gap and using MC pick up and knit 3 sts, *MC k1, CC k1; rep from * around, join to work in the round and place m to indicate beg of rnd—24 (28, 32) sts.

Work even, knitting all sts in color that they are (continuing stripe patt) and incorporating picked up sts into striped patt until thumb measures 1¾ (2, 2) in./4.5 (5, 5) cm from pickup rnd.

Dec Rnd: Using MC only (cut CC) *ssk; rep from * around—12 (14, 16) sts.

Knit 1 rnd.

Dec Rnd: *Ssk; rep from * around—6 (7, 8) sts.

Cut yarn leaving a 6 in./15 cm tail, thread through rem sts using a tapestry needle, pull tight and weave in end.

Right Mitten Thumb

Place 21 (25, 29) sts onto dpns, beg at gap and using MC pick up and knit 3 sts, *CC k1, MC k1; rep from * around, join to work in the round and place m to indicate beg of rnd—24 (28, 32) sts.

Work even, knitting all sts in color that they are (continuing stripe patt) and incorporating picked-up sts into striped patt until thumb measures 1¾ (2, 2) in./4.5 (5, 5) cm from pickup rnd.

Dec Rnd: Using CC only (cut MC) *ssk; rep from * around—12 (14, 16) sts.

Knit 1 rnd.

Dec Rnd: *Ssk; rep from * around—6 (7, 8) sts.

Cut yarn leaving a 6 in./15 cm tail, thread through rem sts using a tapestry needle, pull tight and weave in end.

Finishing

Weave in any loose ends; wet block mittens to set shape and size.

Ferndale Pullover

Geometric lines of stranded colorwork patterning are crossed over each other creating a confluence of pattern, texture, color, and shaping in the yoke of the Ferndale Pullover. The plain stockinette body and simple faced hems are the perfect complement to the unusual and stunning yoke.

For this pattern, I wanted to contrast the detailed yoke pattern with a plain main body and hints of contrast color in a folded and seamed hem. I was thinking about the deep woods of the temperate rainforest when I designed this pullover. We visited the Olympic Peninsula a few years ago as a family, and the depth of the vegetation within the forests there is staggering. This stitch pattern is inspired by the movement of the shadows on the forest floor, deep blue with hints of green that flow over and around each other in that strange organic geometry of nature.

Be Brave level/Experienced: This pattern has intricate patterning on the Adventure Cable such as crossed stitches or stranded colorwork stitches.

Finished Sizes
34 (38, 42, 46, 50) (54, 58, 62, 66, 70) in./86.5 (96.5, 106.5, 117, 127) (137, 147.5, 157.5, 167.5, 178) cm bust circumference
Shown in size 46, modeled with 2 in./5 cm of positive ease.

Yarn
Plymouth Yarn Company Worsted Merino Superwash (#4 medium weight yarn; 100% superwash merino wool; 218 yd./199 m per 4 oz./100 g): 4 (4, 4, 4, 5) (5, 5, 6, 6, 6) skeins #82 Natural Heather (MC), 2 (2, 2, 2, 3) (3, 3, 3, 3, 3) skeins #60 Dress Blues Navy (CC1), 1 skein #84 Fern (CC2)

Needles
US sizes 6 (4.0 mm) and 7 (4.5 mm): 32 in./81 cm circular or straight needles, 16 in./41 cm circular needle, 1 set of 4 double-pointed needles (dpns). Adjust needle size if necessary to obtain the correct gauge.

Notions
1 stitch marker (m), cable needle (cn), tapestry needle

Gauge
20 sts and 26 rnds = 4 in./10 cm in stockinette stitch

20 sts and 24 rnds = 4 in./10 cm over Adventure Cables Pattern

Pattern Notes

This pullover is worked in the round from the bottom up. The hems are worked with a contrast-color facing that is knit on smaller needles with a purl turning rnd. It is best to seam this facing instead of knitting it into the main body, as seaming creates a hem that lies flatter and is less visible. The main body and sleeves are joined after the under-arm shaping bind-off, and short rows are worked to raise the back of the sweater.

It may be necessary to work the stranded patterning with one size larger needle than the main body if the stranded work pulls in.

Alteration Information

Note: Any alterations made may affect yard-age amounts used.

* Adventure Cable repeats for the yoke can be added in multiples of 16. If extra circumference is needed in the bust or upper arm, adding 8 stitches to the bust and 4 stitches to each upper arm is the best course.
* The bottom of each Adventure Cables section starts with a width of 3¼ in./8 cm. If you are adjusting the bottom of the yoke, multiply this width by your intended number of AC sec-tions to calculate the yoke bottom circumference.
* The top of each Adventure Cables section decreases to 1¼ in./3 cm wide. Multiply this by the number of AC sections you are planning in the yoke to calculate the neck circumference. Additional decreases can be worked as long as the remaining stitch count is an even multiple.
* Yoke depth can be adjusted by work-ing more rnds of MC stockinette before the short row shaping or work-ing more repeats of Rows 1–6 of the Adventure Cables Chart.

Stitch Guide

w&t (wrap and turn): Bring yarn between needles to *opposite side* of work, slip next st to right tip, bring yarn between needles to *opposite side* of work, slip st back to left tip, turn work.

Adventure Cables Stitch Guide

Note: For this pattern, a cable needle is required to complete the Adventure Cables.

AC1: 7/1/7 RC with cn: Slip 8 sts to cn and hold in back, MC k2, CC1 k1, MC k1, CC1 k1, MC k2; slip last stitch from cn to left tip, MC k1; then MC k1, [CC1 k1, MC k2] twice, CC1 k1 from cn. *See Photo Tutorial on page 192.*

AC2: 5/5 RC with cn: Slip 5 sts to cn and hold in back, MC k1, CC1 k1, MC k2, CC1 k1, and then [MC k1, CC1 k1] twice, MC k1 from cn.

INSTRUCTIONS

Main Body

Using smaller needles and CC1, CO 170 (190, 210, 230, 250) (270, 290, 310, 330, 350) sts, join to work in the rnd and pm to indicate beg of rnd.

Knit all rnds until piece measures 1 in./ 2.5 cm from cast-on edge.

Change to MC, cut CC1.

Next Rnd: Knit 1 rnd.

Turning Rnd: Purl 1 rnd.

Change to larger needles.

Work in stockinette (knitting all rnds) until piece measures 16 in./40.5 cm from Turning Rnd.

Armhole Shaping Rnd: K77 (84, 90, 96, 105) (114, 123, 131, 139, 146) sts, BO 8 (11, 15, 19, 20) (21, 22, 24, 26, 29) sts, k76 (83, 89, 95, 104) (113, 122, 130, 138, 145), BO rem sts—77 (84, 90, 96, 105) (114, 123, 131, 139, 146) sts on both front and back.

Place all sts onto a holder or waste yarn.

Sleeves

Using smaller dpns and CC1 CO 43 (43, 45, 45, 47) (47, 49, 49, 51, 51) sts, join to work in the rnd and pm to indicate beg of rnd.

Knit all rnds until piece measures 1 in./ 2.5 cm from cast-on edge.

Change to MC, cut CC1.

Next Rnd: Knit 1 rnd.

Turning Rnd: Purl 1 rnd.

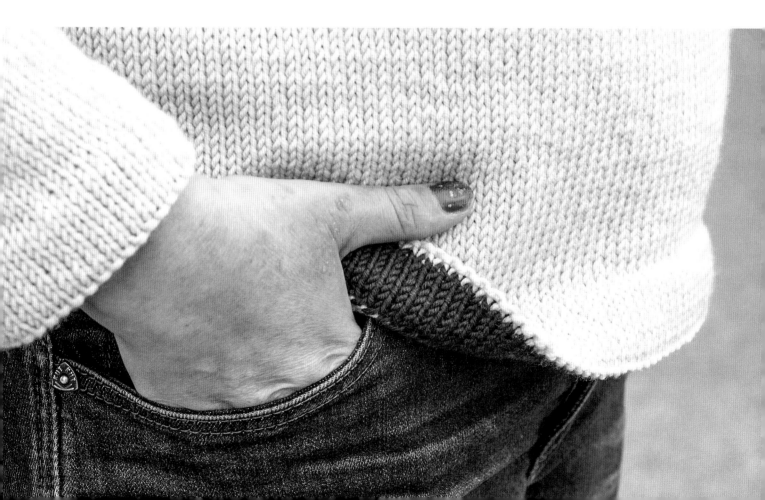

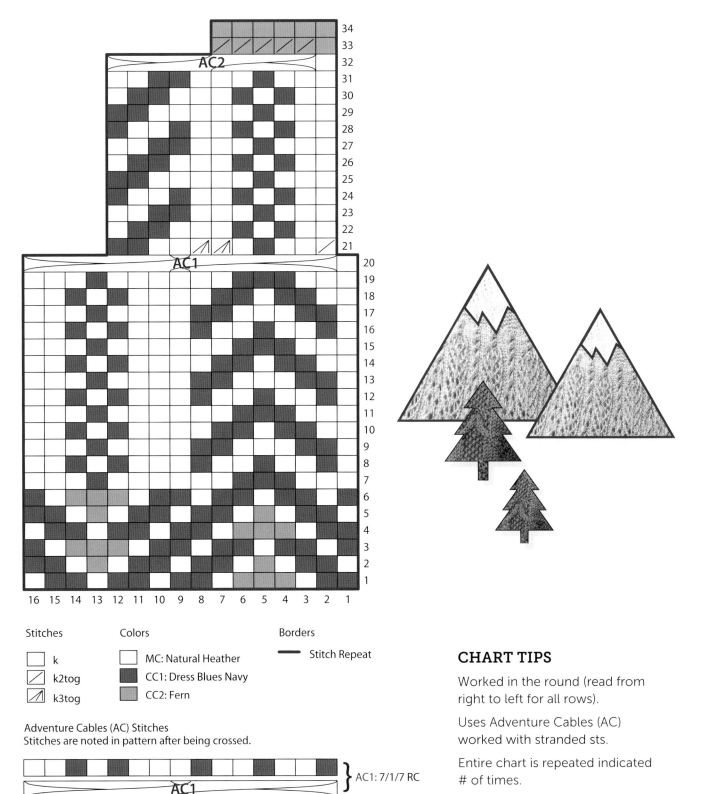

Stitches

☐ k
⬕ k2tog
⬕ k3tog

Adventure Cables (AC) Stitches
Stitches are noted in pattern after being crossed.

Colors

☐ MC: Natural Heather
◼ CC1: Dress Blues Navy
◼ CC2: Fern

Borders

— Stitch Repeat

AC1: 7/1/7 RC

AC2: 5/5 RC

CHART TIPS

Worked in the round (read from right to left for all rows).

Uses Adventure Cables (AC) worked with stranded sts.

Entire chart is repeated indicated # of times.

Work each stitch with color indicated within square.

Change to size 7 (4.5 mm) needles.

Work in stockinette (knitting all rnds) until piece measures 1¼ in./3 cm from Turning Rnd.

Inc Rnd: K1, M1L, knit to last stitch, M1R, K1—2 sts increased.

Rep Inc Rnd every 17 (13, 10, 8, 6) (5, 4, 4, 4, 4) rnds, 5 (7, 9, 12, 15) (19, 22, 23, 23, 25) more times—55 (59, 65, 71, 79) (87, 95, 97, 99, 103) sts.

Work even if necessary until sleeve measures 17 (17, 17¼, 17¼, 17½) (17½, 17¾, 17¾, 18, 18) in./43 (43, 44, 44, 44.5) (44.5, 45, 45, 45.5, 45.5) cm.

Next Rnd: Knit to last 4 (6, 8, 10, 10) (11, 11, 12, 13, 15) sts, BO 8 (11, 15, 19, 20) (21, 22, 24, 26, 29) sts removing marker—47 (48, 50, 52, 59) (66, 73, 73, 73, 74) sts.

Place all sts onto a holder or waste yarn and knit second Sleeve.

Yoke

Joining Rnd: Place Main Body Sts onto size 7 (4.5 mm) 32 in./81 cm circular needle, reattach yarn, [knit across 77 (84, 90, 96, 105) (114, 123, 131, 139, 146) sts from Main Body, pm, knit across 47 (48, 50, 52, 59) (66, 73, 73, 73, 74) sts from Sleeve, pm] twice. Last marker is beg of rnd marker—248 (264, 280, 296, 328) (360, 388, 408, 424, 440) sts.

Knit 2 (4, 6, 6, 8) (10, 12, 14, 16, 18) rnds even.

Short Rows
Row 1: Knit to 10 sts before 2nd marker, w&t.

Row 2: Purl to 10 sts before 3rd marker (this is the third marker from the needle tips at this moment and the third marker placed in the joining rnd), w&t.

Short Row 3: Knit to 10 sts before last wrapped stitch, w&t.

Short Row 4: Purl to 10 sts before last wrapped stitch, w&t.

Rep Short Rows 3–4 once more.

Next Row: Knit to beg of rnd m, sm, knit 1 rnd working in wraps.

Decreases
Dec Rnd: [K1, k2tog, knit to 3 sts before m, ssk, k1] 4 times—240 (256, 272, 288, 320) (352, 384, 400, 416, 432) sts.

Knit 1 rnd even.

Attach CC2, do not cut MC.

Using CC2 knit 2 rnds even, removing all but the beg of rnd marker.

Attach CC1, do not cut MC or CC2.

Work Adventure Cables Chart 15 (16, 17, 18, 20) (22, 24, 25, 26, 27) times around yoke, progressing through Rnds 1–34—90 (96, 102, 108, 120) (132, 144, 150, 156, 162) sts. Cut CC2 after Rnd 6 of Adventure Cables Chart is complete, cont chart with MC and CC1.

Cut CC1.

Sizes 34 (38, 42, 46, 50) in./86 (97, 107, 117, 127) cm only: Using MC knit 2 rnds.

Sizes 54 (58, 62) in./137 (147, 157) cm only: Using MC knit 1 rnd.

Final Decrease Rnds
Use MC for these rnds.

Size 54 in./137 cm only: [K9, k2tog] 11 times—120 sts.

Sizes 58 (62, 66, 70) in./147.5 (157.5, 167.5, 178) cm only: [K4, k2tog] 24 (24, 26, 27) times, knit to end of rnd if necessary—120 (126, 130, 135) sts.

Sizes 66 (70) in./167.5 (178) cm only: [K30 (13), k2tog] 4 (9) times, knit to end of rnd if necessary—126 (126) sts.

Collar
Reattach CC2, cut MC.

Using CC2, knit 1 rnd.

Next Rnd: *K1, p1; rep from * around.

Rep last rnd 2 more times. Change to smaller 16 in./41 cm circular needle, rep last rnd 2 more times. BO all sts in patt.

Finishing
Seam underarm openings and work in any loose ends using tapestry needle. Seam hem facings by turning work under at purl row/turning row and seaming on inside using whipstitch and MC.

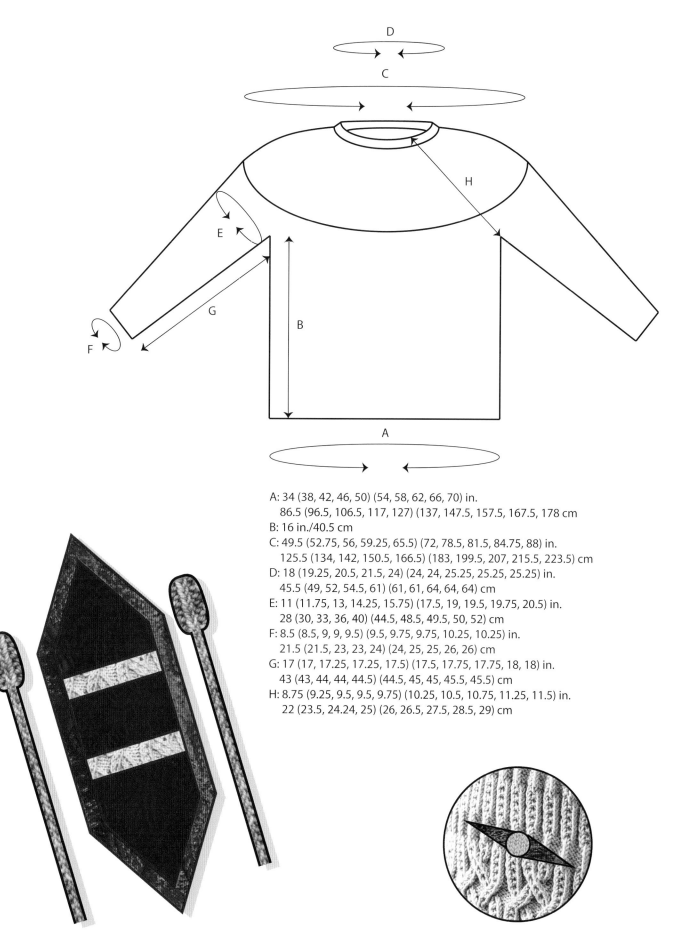

A: 34 (38, 42, 46, 50) (54, 58, 62, 66, 70) in.
   86.5 (96.5, 106.5, 117, 127) (137, 147.5, 157.5, 167.5, 178 cm

B: 16 in./40.5 cm

C: 49.5 (52.75, 56, 59.25, 65.5) (72, 78.5, 81.5, 84.75, 88) in.
   125.5 (134, 142, 150.5, 166.5) (183, 199.5, 207, 215.5, 223.5) cm

D: 18 (19.25, 20.5, 21.5, 24) (24, 24, 25.25, 25.25, 25.25) in.
   45.5 (49, 52, 54.5, 61) (61, 61, 64, 64, 64) cm

E: 11 (11.75, 13, 14.25, 15.75) (17.5, 19, 19.5, 19.75, 20.5) in.
   28 (30, 33, 36, 40) (44.5, 48.5, 49.5, 50, 52) cm

F: 8.5 (8.5, 9, 9, 9.5) (9.5, 9.75, 9.75, 10.25, 10.25) in.
   21.5 (21.5, 23, 23, 24) (24, 25, 25, 26, 26) cm

G: 17 (17, 17.25, 17.25, 17.5) (17.5, 17.75, 17.75, 18, 18) in.
   43 (43, 44, 44, 44.5) (44.5, 45, 45, 45.5, 45.5) cm

H: 8.75 (9.25, 9.5, 9.5, 9.75) (10.25, 10.5, 10.75, 11.25, 11.5) in.
   22 (23.5, 24.24, 25) (26, 26.5, 27.5, 28.5, 29) cm

TUTORIAL: How to Work the Stranded Adventure Cables with a Cable Needle

The Ferndale Pullover is worked with a stranded Adventure Cables yoke that crosses vertical columns of geometric patterning to create a graphic and textured yoke. The finished patterning is a bit of an optical illusion with the geometric chevrons and checkers flowing over each other and the negative space between them becoming the defining edge of each cable. It is recommended to work this cable with a cable needle.

On the chart, the first Adventure Cable (AC1) for the Ferndale Pullover is worked over 15 sts on Round 20. This cable has a single stitch in the middle of the two sets of 7 sts that cross; this single stitch helps to prevent a large gap in the middle of the cable.

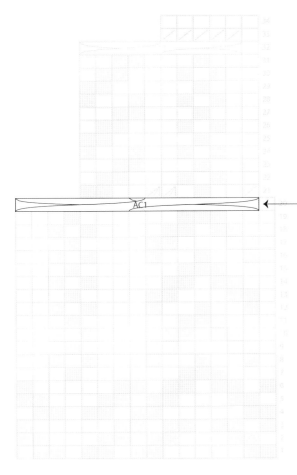

The center sitch in this cable remains in the center; the first 7 stitches and the last 7 stitches are crossed over each other while this stitch is stationary.

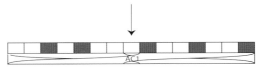

On the chart the first Adventure Cable for the Ferndale Pullover is noted over 15 stitches. On the AC key above we can see that these stitches are worked in a stranded pattern noted above the cable after the stitches are crossed.

1. On Rnd 20, work Stitch 1. The next 15 sts will be used for the Adventure Cable. Slip the first 8 sts onto the cable needle and hold in back.

2. Bring both yarns between the active needle and the cable needle.

3. Work MC k2, CC1 k1, MC k1, CC1 k1, MC k2 across the next 7 sts on the left tip. Below you can see the cable needle in the back of the work holding the first 8 sts and the first 2 sts being worked with the MC on the active needles.

4. Now the 7 sts from the active needle have been worked across.

5. Slip the last stitch from the cable needle to the left tip.

6. Bring the left tip to the left to work across.

7. Knit this stitch with the MC; it is now on the right needle tip.

8. Bring the yarns back between the needles to the right.

9. Slip the rem 7 sts from the cable needle to the left tip.

10. Now all rem 7 sts are on the left tip; work across them as MC k1, [CC1 k1, MC k2] twice, CC1 k1.

11. And the finished Adventure Cable.

Abbreviations

AC Adventure Cable(s)

beg beginning; begin; begins

BO bind off

CC contrasting color

cm centimeter(s)

cn cable needle

CO cast on

cont continue(s); continuing

dec(s) decrease(s); decreasing

dpn(s) double-pointed needle(s)

est established

foll following; follows

inc increase(s); increasing

k knit

k2tog knit two stitches together

kwise knitwise

LC left cross

LT left twist

m marker(s)

MC main color

mm millimeter(s)

M1R (L) make one right (left) increase

p purl

p2tog purl two stitches together

patt(s) pattern(s)

pm place marker

pwise purlwise

RC right cross

rem remain(s); remaining

rep repeat(s); repeating

rib ribbing

rnd(s) round(s)

RS right side

RT right twist

sl slip

sl st slip stitch (slip 1 stitch purlwise unless otherwise indicated)

sm slip marker

ssk [slip 1 kwise] 2 times, insert left needle into fronts of these 2 stitches and work them together through back loops (decrease)

st(s) stitch(es)

St st stockinette stitch

tbl through back loop(s)

tog together

w&t wrap and turn

WS wrong side

wyib with yarn in back

wyif with yarn in front

yo yarnover

* repeat from starting point (i.e., repeat from *)

( ) alternate measurements and/or instructions

[ ] instructions that are to be worked as a group a specified number of times

Yarn Sources

Berroco Yarn
1 Tupperware Dr., Suite 4, N. Smithfield, RI 02896-6815
www.berroco.com/

Plymouth Yarn Company
500 Lafayette St., Bristol, PA 19007
www.plymouthyarn.com/

Sweet Georgia Yarns
408 East Kent Ave. S, #110, Vancouver, BC V5X 2X7, Canada
https://sweetgeorgiayarns.com/

Valley Yarns, WEBS—America's Yarn Store
6 Industrial Pkwy., Easthampton, MA 01027
www.yarn.com/

Huge Thanks to All My Gorgeous Models and Photography Helpers!

Courtney Clark

Ivory Coghlan

Abbey Crawford

Abby Jones-Van Eyck

Kathleen Cubley

Gretchen Cunningham

Norah Jones-Van Eyck

Dani Davis

Gerda Porter

Sarah Magney

Mimi McClellan

Kris Rubert

RaeAnn Nolander

Katie Storo

Camp Projects

KNIT BRAVELY

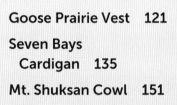
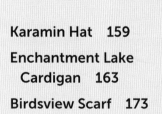